The Little Book God Wants the World to Read

by Raymond S. Porter

 TRILOGY

The Tell-All Book: The Little Book God Wants the World to Read
Trilogy Christian Publishers A Wholly Owned Subsidiary of Trinity Broadcasting Network
2442 Michelle Drive Tustin, CA 92780
Copyright © 2022 by Raymond S. Porter
All scripture quotations are taken from the King James Version of the Bible. Public domain.
No part of this book may be reproduced, stored in a retrieval system, or transmitted by any means without written permission from the author. All rights reserved. Printed in the USA.
Rights Department, 2442 Michelle Drive, Tustin, CA 92780.
Trilogy Christian Publishing/TBN and colophon are trademarks of Trinity Broadcasting Network.
Cover design by: Lauren Gomez
For information about special discounts for bulk purchases, please contact Trilogy Christian Publishing.
Manufactured in the United States of America
10 9 8 7 6 5 4 3 2 1
Library of Congress Cataloging-in-Publication Data is available.
ISBN: 978-1-68556-581-7
E-ISBN: 978-1-68556-582-4

Table of Contents

INTRODUCTION	1
THE TRUTH ABOUT HOMOSEXUALITY AND SAME-SEX MARRIAGE	5
ABORTION	41
CRIME	57
THE ECONOMY	73
RACISM IN AMERICA	91
POLITICS	121
FAITH AND RELIGION IN AMERICA	129
FINAL WORDS	151
ABOUT THE AUTHOR	155

INTRODUCTION

Greetings, in the matchless name of Jesus Christ. Back in the early 1980s, Jesus Christ appeared to me in a dream. He was standing on a mountaintop, wearing a long, white robe, with His arms stretched out toward me, signifying "come to me." I felt unworthy to walk to Him, so I crawled all the way to the summit. When I got there, I saw huge serpents slithering out of the rocks around His feet. He continued to motion to me with stretched-out arms, "Don't be afraid. I will protect you." So, this was my calling to serve Him, with the assurance even though the enemy will try to hinder me, He will always be there to lead, guide, and protect me. I accepted His invitation to serve Him, not knowing my purpose in life, but as time went on and through many trials and tests, He began to reveal His plan for my life piece by piece and a little at a time. Now I unfold part of my purpose in this timely prophetic message, *The Tell-All Book: The Little Book God Wants the World to Read*. I challenge you to be open-minded to what the Spirit of God is saying to you, to receive your blessing.

This is a tell-all book to tell the whole truth and nothing but the truth, so help me, God.

The purpose of this book is not to offend. I ask that you please read the entire book before you make an opinion about it or me. This book is written to expose the truth on many issues looming over us and help unite a divided country and serve as a reference to God's Holy Word concerning these topics for years to come. My prayer is that by reading it, you will find the answers to life, love, joy, peace, and happiness. Above all, I hope you become enlightened to the knowledge of God's saving grace and that many will repent and receive salvation.

Second Chronicles 7:14 says:

> *If my people, which are called by my name, shall humble themselves, and pray, and seek my face, and turn from their wicked ways; then will I hear from heaven, and will forgive their sin, and will heal their land.*

Yes, repentance equals to personal salvation and prosperity of a nation.

There may be some who reject the message and the messenger. But let it be clear: I'm not sent to please men. If I seek to please men, then how can I please God? My duty as God's servant is to please Him and speak only what is written in His Word. I am simply the deliveryman of the message, so if you don't like the message, that's between you and God; don't blame me. I believe many people will be transformed after reading this book because they have come into the knowledge of the truth; the Word of God says, *"And ye shall know the truth, and the truth shall make you free"* (John 8:32). I am sure after reading this book, some will have ill feelings, and it won't be because I don't love you, but because I have told you the truth, and sometimes the truth hurts. Or perhaps I am misunderstood by some. Yet, there will be many who will appreciate this book and be thankful that someone loved me enough to tell me the truth about the subjects you are about to read. The Bible says, *"A true witness delivereth souls: but a deceitful witness speaketh lies"* (Proverbs 14:25). This book is simply about telling the truth in love and not hate. I am sure you have heard of tough love with more emphasis on love? Even though sometimes the truth hurts, it is necessary to deliver a soul. Back in 2002, I became ill. At that time, I was not obedient to God, and I told God if He healed me, I would run for Him and proclaim His truth as He had called me to do. So, here I am, saved, healed, and proclaiming the truth. Hallelujah!

Since 2009, our country has grown even more divided. As a result of this growing division, my intention is to help unite our beloved country as one nation under God, with liberty and justice for all. The reason for this book is best stated in Mark 3:24:

And if a kingdom be divided against itself, that kingdom cannot stand.

I am sure you agree that America is truly divided. Therefore, I invite you, as you read this book, to travel on this voyage of truth with an open mind, and hopefully, after reading it, you will no longer be divided on these issues (after realizing many facts).

I also offer you a simple challenge that's taken from a little passage of scripture in the Bible that I've read many times, but the last time I read it, it stood out more. It's about a woman that Jesus says that for her good work, she would be recognized throughout the world, so I would like to share the story of her good work that she did for Christ. He was so touched by her passion that He says her work would be made known throughout the whole world.

And Jesus said, Let her alone; why trouble ye her? she hath wrought a good work on me. For ye have the poor with you always, and whensoever ye will ye may do them good: but me ye have not always. She hath done what she could: she is come aforehand to anoint my body to the burying. Verily I say unto you, Wheresoever this gospel shall be preached

> *throughout the whole world, this also that she hath done shall be spoken of for a memorial of her.*
>
> Mark 14:6–9

What stood out to me was when Jesus says, "She hath done what she could," she didn't defeat her oppressor, the Roman Empire, to save the Jewish people from slavery and oppression, nor did she build a mega-church for the Jewish people to worship God in. However, one of the things she did was anoint Jesus' body before His burial, which may seem simple and insignificant to some, but to Jesus Christ, it was huge. Her actions and passion for Christ were tremendous to Him, in so much that Christ says her work would be known throughout the world. As one Christian to another, I challenge you to do "what you can do" for Christ to make this world a better place and remember only what we do for Christ shall last forever. Also, sometimes it's the little things that we do for Christ that make a big difference.

Half the proceeds of this book will go to helping the poor, spreading the gospel, and standing up for the voiceless unborn. God bless you, and thank you for your support.

CHAPTER ONE
THE TRUTH ABOUT HOMOSEXUALITY
AND SAME-SEX MARRIAGE

I would like to start by saying that I am not homophobic and by no means do I condone gay-bashing. Make no mistake, I will not stand by and allow anyone to bash or assault anyone who is gay.

Many gay people are some of the kindest people you can meet, and they are welcome at our church with open arms. It is wrong to discriminate against them. I am one who genuinely loves gay people as I love anyone else. God loves homosexuals as much as he loves heterosexuals. But God does not love their sins and the practice of homosexuality for the same reasons; He is not pleased with the sins and practice of fornication, which is having sex out of wedlock. God also loves heterosexuals, but He hates the practice of committing adultery against His Holy Word. In 1 John 5:17, Christ talks about sins that are not unto death. *"All unrighteousness is sin: and there is a sin not unto death"* (1 Corinthians 6:9–11). Here He states the sins that are sins unto death that would damn the soul.

> *Know ye not that the unrighteous shall not inherit the kingdom of God? Be not deceived: neither fornicators, nor idolaters, nor adulterers, nor effeminate, nor abusers of themselves with mankind, Nor thieves, nor covetous, nor drunkards, nor revilers, nor extortioners, shall inherit the kingdom of God. And such were some of you: but ye*

are washed, but ye are sanctified, but ye are justified in the name of the Lord Jesus, and by the Spirit of our God.

These are the words of Apostle Paul to the church of Corinth, warning the Corinthians of deadly sins. In this biblical passage, the particular sin of being effeminate is when men have the characteristic traits of a woman. God clearly points out that no effeminate person will inherit the kingdom of God, meaning whosoever practices homosexuality cannot enter heaven; the same goes for adulterers.

Now the beauty of this passage of scripture is that it shows God's impartiality. He says heterosexuals who commit adultery and fornication will not inherit the kingdom of God either. This stands as one of the reasons that this chapter must be written. As pastors, we are often ridiculed for preaching and teaching against homosexuality, but no one condemns us as God's servants when we preach and teach against heterosexuals who practice the evils of adultery and fornication.

Why is it that we get criticized for preaching against homosexuality and not against adulterous heterosexual behavior? Because people assume that we are homophobic. I always say to assume something about someone is the mother of all evil. We are merely doing our jobs as men of the cloth. So, why aren't we also called adultery-phobic or fornication-haters?

It is part of our calling to preach the truth to all, regardless of one's gender or sexual preference. As you can see in this passage of scripture, Paul says, *"And such were some of you…"*

And such were some of you: but ye are washed, but ye are sanctified, but ye are justified in the name of the Lord Jesus, and by the Spirit of our God.

1 Corinthians 6:11

In layman's terms, meaning past tense, they forsook all those practices that were in direct disobedience to God's Word. They repented and got saved. Therefore, you cannot live the lifestyle of a homosexual and be a Christian, just as one cannot live the lifestyle of an adulterer and be a Christian. A true Christian is supposed to imitate Christ. This imitation requires us to walk in this world the way Jesus walked; therefore, we should strive to live holy every day. Why? Because in 1 Peter 1:16, it states:

"Because it is written, Be ye holy; for I am holy."

Now let us look deeper into this masquerade of a lifestyle, disguising itself as innocent and harmless, that former President Obama tried to make it mainstream in society, which I will discuss later. This is part of Satan's diabolical plot to bring God's judgment upon America. Please take no offense because it is not my intention. It is my *job* to warn all who go against God's Holy Word that they are putting themselves in great danger of God's wrath, whether they be kings, presidents, rulers, judges, or clergymen. No one should teach contrary to God's commandments.

Let us weigh in on the Supreme Court case hearing concerning the Colorado baker who refused to make a celebration wedding cake for a gay couple, who sued him on the grounds of discrimination. This lawsuit was unfounded because it was his godly conviction that prevented him from being a participant on such an occasion, not discrimination; he's protected under what is known as conscientious objection. He made it very clear that he would serve anyone, regardless of who they were. He made it known that he serves all people, but not in a case such as this. Now, if he would not sell his products to all customers, then that would be discrimination. However, for him to decline to custom design something using his art skills to create something that goes against his faith is not discrimination. What if a tiger owner requested that an animal rights activist T-shirt business owner personally design him a T-shirt image of him and his tiger locked up in a cage while posing with a chair and holding a whip in his hand? Is that a fair request knowing that he opposes such behavior? However, the T-shirt business owner refused to create the artwork on the T-shirt for the paying customer due to his belief that tigers should roam freely in their natural environment, and unequivocally refused to advocate warehousing wild animals and afflicting them with whips, and chose to politely decline his special request, yet have a willingness to sell him anything in his shop or design him something else. Should the tiger's owner have the right to sue the T-shirt business owner and animal rights activist's and force him out of business and lose his livelihood simply because he refuses to participate in something that he truly believes is wrong? Absolutely not. He should seek out a T-shirt business elsewhere whose beliefs and passion aren't as sensitive as the animal rights activists are.

What the baker is saying is, I can't help you with anything that goes against my faith, especially the sin of sodomy/same-sex marriage. This, for him, is a type of aiding and abetting a sin, which shouldn't be taken personally if reasonably understood. Here is a scenario of what the baker was saying: take two bank robbers, and one physically goes inside and robs the bank, and the other one is the watchman and getaway driver. If they both get caught, both will be charged even though the getaway driver did not rob the bank, but because he was an accomplice to the crime, he's just as guilty. I feel that the Colorado baker did not want to be an accomplice to something that's illegal in the eyes of God and perhaps be charged by God for indirectly condoning the evil practice of same-sex marriage. What the gay couple should have done was simply go to a baker with no conscientious objection to accommodate them instead of turning this into something that it's not, such as a so-called discrimination case.

The reason I have written with such concern about this matter is that hopefully, someday, the gay community will get it. It's not anything personal against them nor discriminatory. We are simply obeying God and exercising our freedom of religion. Even if the Supreme Court takes away the rights to refuse service due to conscientious objection, we must still obey God rather than man, regardless of the consequence. With all due respect to the Honorable Supreme Court Justices, I would like to remind you that you are the last stand for moral justice in America. We the people look to you to help carve out a moral society that's pleasing to God, not man, which represents who we are for generations to come, and not to fear God's creation (man) but your creator God when you make your rulings. Also, remember, you have a Judge over you, whom we all must answer. Let it be known that we as Christians love the gay community, but there are certain things that we cannot accept in the gay community world. Understandably, even though you honestly believe that same-sex marriage is okay, and of course, you have the right to believe and do whatever you like, so, since we don't see it that way, please afford us the same respect. Many believers across the world see same-sex marriage as sinful and in direct disobedience against God's Holy Word, so why not respectfully respect our Christian beliefs and stop trying to force us to accept your belief in the sin of sodomy. We see the government trying to make devout Christians participate in such sinful behavior against their core beliefs. How can the government make you do something that you feel might be damning to your soul? I mean, what's next? Will the government try to force us to denounce Christ? Where does it stop?

I applaud the Colorado baker for standing his ground for God, and may God richly bless him and his family with peace and the assurance that there is more for him than against him. I warn all the pastors that something like this could hit home for many of you. For example, if you run an advertisement that you provide a civil service to officiate events and ceremonies for a small fee, such as weddings for people who don't have a church home, and if a gay couple responds to your ad for your service to marry them, and you refuse due to your religious belief, as crazy as it may sound, the way things are going nowadays this could be grounds for a possible lawsuit against you for discrimination. Please, let me make myself clear, I would not marry a gay couple if someone offered me one billion dollars in cash. And I am sure someone might think I am crazy to turn down that kind of money. My response will be that there's not enough money in the world that will cause me to sell out my faith and my God. That's how much I love and fear God. And for all the prominent preachers with big platforms who refuse to speak out against the madness of same-sex marriage, if you love them, you will tell them the truth in love. The Bible says, *"And ye shall know the truth, and the truth shall make you free"* (John 8:32). If you do not speak the truth, then you are nothing but a hireling, who's merely concerned about your image, popularity, and acceptance, and, above all, your money; therefore, you have received your reward.

One of the biggest misconceptions about the gay rights movement is that it tries to make itself a so-called civil rights issue with high hopes that it can sell this lie to the American people. And that's exactly what Satan wants you to believe. On the contrary, the gay agenda has nothing to do with civil rights. Gays want the right to practice the wickedness of sodomy openly and receive government benefits as well. They want everyone to make light of this behavior. That's why they gave their behavior the name *gay*, which means homosexual, happy, joyful.

Gays appear to be happy, but it's not true happiness. Rather, in the end, it's destruction. I liken it to a farmer who raises pigs for a living; he feeds them plenty of slop and gives them a pen to wallow in and play in the mud. This is heaven to them. They are happy, but they do not realize they're being fattened up for the slaughter.

Look at some of the great entertainers and singers who died as they were sitting on top of the world, having fame, riches, homes, cars, and the best of drugs and alcohol; still, it could not buy them true peace and happiness. They could not overcome their demons, some overdosed on drugs, and others committed suicide—all because they were living outside of God's will. They were being fattened up with the worldly slop of sins and pleasures, all for the destruction and slaughter of their souls. They were good-hearted people whom Satan blinded and led away from God's true Word.

This is the same artificial happiness that most LGBTQ are experiencing, brought about through lots of partying and constant use of drugs, alcohol, and sexual immorality that's never satisfying. For some, this leads to chronic depression, occasional suicidal thoughts and tendencies, and an overwhelming feeling of confusion and rejection.

Some gay people live a quiet life with their partners. They work hard, play by the rules, and achieve the American dream. But true happiness eludes them, especially if they know the truth of God's Word. Homosexuality is rooted in ancient evil spirits that work through mankind. At one time, the practice escalated so much that God destroyed two major cities in the Old Testament called Sodom and Gomorrah.

In Genesis 19:1–7, God sent two angels to warn Lot, Abraham's nephew, to get out of Sodom and Gomorrah because God planned to destroy both cities. So, God rained down fire and brimstone from heaven because the cities were corrupt with the perversion of same-sex activity.

The story tells of how homosexual men went to Lot's home to take the angels by force to sodomize them. Lot pleaded with them not to do such a wicked thing with his guests, not knowing they were angels sent to destroy the cities. The story reads as follows:

> *And there came two angels to Sodom at even; and Lot sat in the gate of Sodom: and Lot seeing them rose up to meet them; and he bowed himself with his face toward the ground; And he said, Behold now, my lords, turn in, I pray you, into your servant's house, and tarry all night, and wash your feet, and ye shall rise up early, and go on your ways. And they said, Nay; but we will abide in the street all night. And he pressed upon them greatly; and they turned in unto him, and entered into his house; and he made them a feast, and did bake unleavened bread, and they did eat. But before they lay down, the men of the city, even the men of Sodom, compassed the house round, both old and young, all the people from every quarter: And they called unto Lot, and said unto him, Where are the men which came in to thee this night? bring them out unto us, that we may know them. And Lot went out at the door unto them, and shut the door after him, And said, I pray you, brethren, do not so wickedly. Behold*

now, I have two daughters which have not known man; let me, I pray you, bring them out unto you, and do ye to them as is good in your eyes: only unto these men do nothing; for therefore came they under the shadow of my roof. And they said, Stand back. And they said again, This one fellow came in to sojourn, and he will needs be a judge: now will we deal worse with thee, than with them. And they pressed sore upon the man, even Lot, and came near to break the door. But the men put forth their hand, and pulled Lot into the house to them, and shut to the door. And they smote the men that were at the door of the house with blindness, both small and great: so that they wearied themselves to find the door.

Genesis 19:1–11

Sodom is where the word *sodomy* comes from, meaning abnormal sexual behavior. It is where we get the term *sodomy rape*, having sex with the same sex. It's not normal for a man to put his penis into another man's anus. The anus is the opening of the rectum, which stool passes through. The penis mixing in human feces, blood, and semen can spread diseases such as HIV/AIDS. If this sexual proclivity is so innocent, why then can it lead to such sickness and horrible deaths caused by AIDS? For someone to do this isn't normal. It's clearly not the individual but spiritual forces of darkness working in them, known as demonic spirits, which influence such behavior.

Here is a statement by the late Prince R. Nelson, the famous guitar player "Prince," made to *The New Yorker's* Claire Hoffman in 2008 on the issue of homosexuality and God.

When asked about his perspective on social issues—gay marriage, abortion—Prince tapped his Bible and said, "God came to earth and saw people sticking it wherever and doing it with whatever, and he just cleared it all out. He was, like, 'Enough.'"

Here you find Prince denouncing this lifestyle with the understanding that God is against it.

The repercussion of the practice alone proves it is not of God. If it is ok, why is it so destructive? Nor is it God's plan for procreation. How can two women have a baby, or two men, for that matter? It is sexually impossible.

I sometimes see two women together, one dressing to resemble a man, or so-called "*stud*," and the other as a lady, or so-called "*fem*," but they will never be able to produce a child simply because it's not God's plan for mankind. One can become a surrogate or adopt a child, but that adds confusion to the child. In plain language, this is an abomination in the eyes of God.

According to the Holy Word of God in Leviticus 20:13:

> *If a man also lie with mankind, as he lieth with a woman, both of them have committed an abomination: they shall surely be put to death; their blood shall be upon them.*

Here, God is referring to two men sleeping together, so it is clearly an abomination to God, meaning it is a disgusting, vile, dislikeable, abhorrent, and shameful action. The Bible term "put to death" in the Old Testament was under the time period of the Law, but now we're in the New Testament time period, which is known as a dispensation or time period called Grace and Mercy. Therefore, God does not support such punishment of putting someone to death for sin. For example, in the Old Testament, they executed people for committing adultery, but in this age of grace and mercy, God does not sanction executions for adultery. For example, there was a woman that was caught in the act of adultery and the Scribes and the Pharisees, who were some of the prominent spiritual rulers of that time, wanted to put her to death because, under the law of Moses, an adulterer was sentenced to death. It reads as follows:

> *Jesus went unto the mount of Olives. And early in the morning he came again into the temple, and all the people came unto him; and he sat down, and taught them. And the scribes and Pharisees brought unto him a woman taken in adultery; and when they had set her in the midst, They say unto him, Master, this woman was taken in adultery, in the very act. Now Moses in the law commanded us, that such should be stoned: but what sayest thou? This they said, tempting him, that they might have to accuse him. But Jesus stooped down, and with his finger wrote on the ground, as though he heard them not. So when they continued asking him, he lifted up himself, and said unto them, He that is without sin among you, let him first cast a stone at her. And again he stooped down, and wrote on the ground. And they which heard it, being convicted by their own conscience, went out one by one, beginning at the eldest, even unto the last: and Jesus was left alone, and the woman standing in the midst. When Jesus had lifted up himself, and saw none but the woman, he said unto her, Woman, where are those thine accusers? hath no man condemned thee? She said, No man, Lord. And Jesus said unto her, Neither do I condemn thee: go, and sin no more.*

John 8:1–11

Thanks be to God that we are no longer under the Law but spared by the Grace and Mercy of God by faith and repentance.

Let us get back to Satan's diabolical plot, in which former President Obama and some of his appointed judges tried to force this wicked agenda down the throats of many God-fearing Christians who are opposed to it.

Just because we don't agree with you doesn't mean we are haters. Please, stop trying to make us accept your beliefs. What about our beliefs and feelings? Their agenda is a one-way view.

With no regard for how others feel, it's like a gay couple telling a preacher, "You are going to marry me and my partner whether you like it or not; if not, I'm going to sue you and your church and take all its assets," and that's not right. To us, that's like we are damned if we do and damned if we don't; there are some people and companies that try to cancel certain people for not embracing their belief in such practices, which is mean-spirited. By the way, you can't cancel anyone who stands on and lives by the Holy Word of God. Let me be clear: when it comes to obeying man over God, there is no contest with me; I stand with God every single time. The most sickening part is when I hear people compare the gay agenda to the historical civil rights struggle, wherein so many Blacks and Whites paid the ultimate sacrifice for freedom, equality, opportunity, and justice for all. Our ancestors and forefathers of this great country fought politically, physically, and spiritually, so all Americans might enjoy the same rights. The Declaration of Independence states:

> *"We hold these truths to be self-evident, that all men are created equal, that they are endowed by their Creator with certain unalienable Rights, that among these are Life, Liberty, and the pursuit of Happiness."*

What you just read was established to enforce fair rights for all, not to promote sin and the gay agenda. I am asking this country to *please stop* comparing the Civil Rights Act to the wickedness of the gay movement. It is very insulting, especially to the Black community. If I had to describe it, it would be like trying to compare Adolf Hitler to a Saint of God. There are absolutely no comparisons at all.

Another sick comparison is equating the struggle of legalizing interracial marriage to same-sex marriage. They try to feed off our emotions by comparing civil rights movements to their personal sinful agenda. Sorry, we're not going to fall for that one. The scripture spells out clearly that the deeds of homosexuality are an abomination. Therefore, it was wrong in the eyes of God yesterday, it is wrong today, and it will be wrong tomorrow. God never said interracial marriage was wrong, in the sense of one's pigmentation or the color of one's skin. It's a prejudicial attitude by mankind that opposes interracial marriage; God does not oppose interracial marriage; it's mankind who has a problem with it, not God.

As for viewing interracial marriage from a biblical perspective, in the Old Testament, God opposed the Jews from mixing races because marrying strangers outside of the Jewish faith would cause them to learn the heathen's ways and turn the Jews' hearts from serving God toward serving false gods and worshiping pagan idols. That's why God, in the Old Testament, forbids Jews from mixed marriages. In this period and time, God doesn't care who you marry or what color their skin is, as long as they are believers and, of course, are of the opposite sex.

My biggest concern with these immoral issues is that we, as a Christian nation, must fix our moral compass. Throughout history, we have found that our government was not the one who fixed it. We saw how former President Obama and his administration were too busy trying to write their own histories rather than obeying God. If our leaders do not wake up, they will one day find themselves on the wrong side of history. Most importantly, if they don't change course, one day, they may realize they have sold their soul just for fame. I repeat; it is my job to warn you.

Seeing as how our government refuses to adjust our moral compass, let us, as fellow Americans, fix it. Just to show you how badly it's broken, I would like to recite the values of the Russian government to make my case. Look at the Russian lower house of parliament, or *Duma*. Here's a country that doesn't claim to be a Christian nation but has been found to be more righteous than we, in this matter. This alone is a testimony against us. One headline reads: *Gay pride fines were to be imposed under a Russian law passed by a vote of 436–0.* Unbelievable. In June 2013, the Associated Press reported that:

> "Russia's lower house approved a bill on Tuesday that will impose fines for anyone who provides information about homosexuality to minors or holds gay pride rallies… The measure is part of an effort to promote traditional Russian values instead of Western liberalism…"

Did you get that? They do not want anything to do with Western marriage customs.

You may Google the article from June 11, 2013, at www. newsmax.com and enter in the search bar "gay pride fines to be imposed under Russian law." Now, I do not believe in such a measure, or any type of punishment for that matter, because man cannot regulate sin or make one stop sinning. Only God's Holy Spirit can convict and turn the hearts of men from the power of darkness to the power of light—from evil to good. No manner of laws can do that, only God's love. The Bible says in Jeremiah:

The LORD hath appeared of old unto me, saying, Yea, I have loved thee with an everlasting love: therefore with lovingkindness have I drawn thee.

Jeremiah 31:3

As I said earlier, God loves gay people, but He opposes their practice, just as most Americans oppose their practices. But the U.S. Supreme Court voted 5–4 in favor of redefining the Defense of Marriage Act. Under the Court's June 2015 ruling, marriages are no longer exclusively between a man and a woman but are now open to the same sex. If you want to call it a marriage, you can, but in God's eyes, this marriage is not recognized.

No matter how much we, as believers, stress this point, you will never see or concur unless you see it through the eyes of God and His Holy Word. It's hard for worldly people to see this because they are of this world and not of God's spiritual world. Here God explains why you cannot see homosexuality is wrong, in 1 John 4:5–6:

> *They are of the world: therefore speak they of the world, and the world heareth them. We are of God: he that knoweth God heareth us; he that is not of God heareth not us. Hereby know we the spirit of truth, and the spirit of error.*

I pray that God will open your eyes because you are in error. God's Word does not change with time and new movements or fads. For God says: *"Heaven and earth shall pass away, but my words shall not pass away"* (Matthew 24:35). The bottom line is that the Supreme Court should not be in the business of promoting and governing sexual immorality because God Himself has already ruled on this matter through His Word. And God's Law is the final Supreme Law and supersedes man's laws. In the end, this has absolutely nothing to do with civil rights. However, if they choose to live such a lifestyle, then let them be.

Again, there was a woman in the Bible who was caught in the act of adultery, which was one of the ultimate immoral sins punishable by death under the Law. But notice, Jesus did not condemn her to death. Instead, He instructed her to go and sin no more. He left her future in her own hands. If she refused to go and repent, Jesus knew she would still face Judgment Day. The Supreme Court has trodden on dangerous ground. So, with that, a warning to the Justices: you could possibly be in danger of eternal judgment just to make history.

The Supreme Court has been wrong in the past on many issues regarding morality and what is Constitutional and Unconstitutional. The Court found itself on the wrong side of history in the case of *Plessy v. Ferguson* in 1896, when it ruled that segregation was legal and that Black people stood as separate but equal. This led the Supreme Court to uphold the state racial segregation law, which was considered a Jim Crow law that subjected Black citizens to inferior treatment. Although years later, in 1954, the Court overturned the law "separate but equal" in the case of *Brown v. Board of Education of Topeka*. And I am happy to say, after 130 years of being wrongfully charged, just recently, the Louisiana Governor John Bel Edwards granted a posthumous pardon on Wednesday, January 5, 2022, for Homer Plessy, who refused in 1892 to leave a Whites-only railcar, has finally received justice.

The Supreme Court was wrong in 1896, just as it was wrong in 2015 on the same-sex marriage decision.

One may ask, "How did we get to this point?" I say we allowed spiritual wickedness and blindness in high places of authority in our courts and judicial systems. The Bible says in Ephesians 6:12:

> *For we wrestle not against flesh and blood, but against principalities, against powers, against the rulers of the darkness of this world, against spiritual wickedness in high places.*

That is why you should be prayerful about who you vote into office; Satan could have appointed these leaders himself to pass laws that help promote evil.

With all due respect, it was sad to see our former President Obama travel to Senegal, Africa, attempting to promote the practice of homosexuality among them. They refused to accept his ideology of same-sex marriage because they fear God. The Bible says in Proverbs 9:10, *"The fear of the LORD is the beginning of wisdom: and the knowledge of the holy is understanding."*

After hearing the African position on this matter, their law prohibits same-sex marriage in certain parts of Africa. However,

I do not believe in any type of persecution or imprisonment against gay people; it's simply wrong because you cannot force immorality change; this change must come from the heart. It is ironic for us to send missionaries and evangelists to them. They should be sending teachers and instructors of God's Word to the U.S. regarding God's law on marriage. Why did former President Barack Obama go to Africa to try to indoctrinate them with his beliefs on same-sex marriage? Maybe because to some people, they seem inferior and unable to write their own constitution. Or there's a belief that they don't know what's best for their own countries. On the contrary, they are much wiser than the U.S. regarding the matter of same-sex marriage.

I think former President Obama should have been focusing on strengthening the economy and visiting poverty-stricken neighborhoods with high unemployment and epidemic crime rates. I believe that Mr. Obama should have focused on issues such as black-on-black crime, joblessness, and homelessness. He should have pushed for a message of hope for the inner cities, like Los Angeles, Detroit, Chicago, and Philadelphia. Yes, it would have been so nice to see our former President Obama involved in something more meaningful than the promotion of sodomy, like helping minorities in inner cities become working-class citizens, taxpayers, and law-abiding citizens instead of promoting the lewd behavior of sodomy which has absolutely nothing to do with civil rights.

If the truth be told, former President Obama did nothing meaningful for the African American community. However, he did appease the gay community and helped push their agenda into law. Especially when he was confronted by the gay community for not supporting them and their agenda during his first term. He was quickly reminded how they raised money for his campaign to help him get elected. So, he made it very clear that he would support their right to marry in his second reelection campaign. So, he went public on ABC's *Good Morning America* in an interview with ABC News Robin Roberts stating his thought process as an "evolution" along with conversations with other people led him to his decision to affirm his support for same-sex marriage. If he had talked with God, he would have gotten a completely different answer. My prayer is that God will open the eyes of our leaders of this great nation because it's like the blind leading the blind.

Now, what bill will they try to pass next in the name of so-called civil rights? Will there be a bill to license sex with animals for those who love to practice bestiality because they feel they have the right to have sex with their pet monkey? The Word of God states in Exodus 22:19, *"Whosoever lieth with a beast shall surely be put to death."*

It was so horrible that God ordered the elders of Israel to put such a person to death who had sex with animals. Of course, that is not the case nowadays, because back then, they were under the Old Law, but now we are under the Grace of God.

From a religious perspective, the act of bestiality is in the same class as the forbidden laws of homosexuality in the Bible. When you study the scriptures, sleeping with animals was wrong then, it is wrong today, and it will be wrong tomorrow. Just like men sleeping with other men is wrong. Even if the Supreme Court were to rule someday that sex with an animal is protected by the Constitution, that would not make it right. It will still be an act of perversion, confusion, and madness, just as with same-sex marriage.

May we continue to focus on the truth of homosexuality? This deadly sin is not new to society. It goes back to the beginning of civilization. It has always been and will always be among us as long as the Lord delays His coming, when He returns to take away the righteous. No one can stop the homosexual movement because of biblical prophecy, which states that, in the last days, it will be like Sodom and Gomorrah. I can't stop it, you can't stop it, and God won't stop it. There must be a willingness for repentance from the heart and as a nation. If not, I hate to think what it will be like in future generations if we don't repent and teach our children what's right and wrong based upon God's Holy Word. May God have mercy on us all. We, as a Christian nation, should not support homosexuality in any form. Homosexuality is like wild grass in a garden. It doesn't need any support to grow; it thrives all by itself.

The Word of God points out clearly how Satan used men to plant bad seeds in a good garden. America is a good garden with values that are based upon God's Word. But the enemy wants to plant bad values in the land like this parable. According to Matthew 13:24–30:

> *Another parable put he forth unto them, saying, The kingdom of heaven is likened unto a man which sowed good seed in his field: But while men slept, his enemy came and sowed tares among the wheat, and went his way. But when the blade was sprung up, and brought forth fruit, then appeared the tares also. So the servants of the householder came and said unto him, Sir, didst not thou sow good seed in thy field? from whence then hath it tares? He said unto them, An enemy hath done this. The servants said unto him, Wilt thou then that we go and gather them up? But he said, Nay; lest while ye gather up the tares, ye root up also the wheat with them. Let both grow together until the harvest: and in the time of harvest I will say to the reapers, Gather ye together first the tares,*

and bind them in bundles to burn them: but gather the wheat into my barn.

Matthew 13:36–40:

Then Jesus sent the multitude away, and went into the house: and his disciples came unto him, saying, Declare unto us the parable of the tares of the field. He answered and said unto them, He that soweth the good seed is the Son of man; The field is the world; the good seed are the children of the kingdom; but the tares are the children of the wicked one; The enemy that sowed them is the devil; the harvest is the end of the world; and the reapers are the angels. As therefore the tares are gathered and burned in the fire; so shall it be in the end of this world.

Clearly, we can see the bad seeds that have been planted directly from this law. However, God will judge it in the end.

I pray that the U.S. government wakes up and sees that it is an instrument of the devil by passing laws of bad seeds that promote homosexuality. Some in the homosexual community will repent, change, and become saved. Unfortunately, others will never change because the Word of God has spoken, and the Word cannot change. He said in the last days, it will be like Sodom and Gomorrah, meaning there will come a time when major cities will be predominantly populated by gays who rule the entire city. They will prosper economically and grow in numbers, but God will not be with them. It will be like the Tower of Babel, where people were full of the spirit of pride and arrogance. Even they themselves have made it known by their slogan: *Gay Pride*. This pride has worked its way into our Armed Forces, putting sin in the camp. Even the nation of Israel—the apple of God's eye—has allowed this evil sin to be practiced openly in its army. They are simply saying, forget God and His Word. We are going to do what the people will us to do, not God. I strongly advise the Israeli army to purge its army of this sin because God is not pleased with such sin in your camp (The Israel Defense Forces). I would like to call your attention to the story of a man named Achan who brought sin into the camp of Israel at the battle of Ai, and God was not with them because of the accursed thing in the camp. You will find this story in Joshua 7:1–26: Israel had committed a trespass when Achan brought in an accursed thing that displeased God, so much that He was not with them during the battle of Ai, where their enemy defeated them shortly after their victory at Jericho. Joshua, Moses' predecessor, who never lost a battle with his army, led the Israelites in their war conquering campaign for the promised land with 100% success. Because of their great leader, who taught them the fear of the Lord, Egypt's slaves became a well-respected and feared army. Yet, Joshua lost a battle because of sin in the camp due to a man who disregarded the Word of the Lord. Therefore, if you want the God of Moses to be with you in future wars, remove the wicked sin of sodomy from your Armed Forces with love and respect.

Let it be known that God will not be with the U.S. Armed Forces in time of battle, particularly against the bear and eagle, until they remove the perversion sins of sodomy from the Armed Forces. Let me make myself clear: former President Trump was most definitely wrong on the Charlottesville tragedy for not initially and sharply condemning the racist fascists, who sought to promote their racist ideology, which only serves to poison and divide our country. But as far as a ban on transgender sex change in the military, he's right. God bless him for having the courage to stand up for what is right by seeking to put an end to all the confusion and problems this policy will bring. Let's look at two major biblical contrasts between two former presidents, Barack Obama and Donald Trump. Here we find that President Obama helped fulfill one of the biggest last-day biblical prophecies by promoting homosexuality. In other words, he helped usher in one of the biblical prophecies of God's Word that speaks of the last days, how it will be like Sodom and Gomorrah, where men were sleeping with men and women with women as they performed all types of sexual acts of perversion. Now, on the other hand, we find President Trump assisted in fulfilling future prophecies by helping solidify Israel's sovereignty when he pushed for Jerusalem to become the capital of Israel. One president helped fulfill a bad prophecy, and the other helped fulfill a good one. I often hear people berating Trump for some things he may have said and done in the past; of course, I don't agree with everything Mr. Trump may have said or done, remember, no one is perfect. However, I do agree with some of his policies, especially his pro-life policy and his willingness to help put an end to abortion. God used former President Trump to nominate conservative judges to the Supreme Court, which recently left in place a Texas law that bans most abortions after six weeks and provided only a narrow path for providers to challenge in federal court what is the nation's most restrictive law on abortion procedures. It was God's great mercy that enabled former President Trump and his brave Supreme Court appointees to save countless innocent babies' lives, and whether you like it or not, God is not through using Mr. Trump, and there will be many women that will later appreciate the abortion ban once they hold their precious little babies in their hands. I encourage future presidents to search the Holy Scriptures and seek counseling from men of God to make sure that the laws they are passing are acceptable with God's will.

Former President Trump's push to stop a policy that allows transgender sex change in the Armed Forces was on point. History has shown that the U.S. Armed Forces uphold high moral standards; allowing such practice will lower the standards. So, putting an end to all sodomy activities will help ensure our Armed Forces are in favor of God during war times. Please remember this is not personal; it's the right thing to do. I share this because I love my brothers and sisters who serve and protect our great country. However, the condoned sin of sodomy puts them out of the will of God. Now, for those who support the LGBTQs in this matter, it's just a matter of do you want to be politically correct or Godly correct. You decide.

This transgender policy will allow taxpayers' money to be used for transgender people's sex changes in the military. One may question the cost, but the financial cost is not the problem: it's all the underlying problems associated with this immoral and ungodly sex change practice that it will create in the U.S. Armed Forces. This will be a sign unto you that the hand of God is against us: when you see the bear smite the eagle. The reason why is according to the Word of God found in Isaiah 59:2:

> *But your iniquities have separated between you and your God, and your sins have hid his face from you, that he will not hear.*

I dreamed many years ago that the bear had defeated the eagle, but only wounding her because she rejected God's Word. We all know that the bear and the eagle represent two nations. This dream will be explained in detail in Chapter 7, titled "Faith and Religion."

I ask all fellow Americans to stand together and reject these bad-seed laws of same-sex marriage. Let us do it in love, not judgmentally, for God's Word has already judged the lifestyle of homosexuality.

Pope Francis made the statement, "If someone is gay and he searches for the Lord and has goodwill, who am I to judge?" This statement is not clear at all. God does not generalize when it comes to right and wrong. No, it is not right to cast judgment on someone to the point of condemnation; no one has a heaven or hell to put anyone in, only God. However, it is clearly okay to tell someone when they are wrong, and we should encourage them to repent. The Pope needs to tell the priests that homosexuality is wrong, point-blank. Having goodwill is one thing, but repenting is another. That is to turn away from sin, to feel such regret for past conduct as to change one's mind regarding it, to be remorseful, and to ask God's forgiveness.

One way to help put an end to the pedophilia problem in the Catholic faith is to allow the priests who do not possess the gift or calling from God to live a life of celibacy to marry. The Apostle Paul had that gift, but he also realized that not everyone does and that it was better to marry than to burn with passion in the flesh and commit sexual immortalities, as he explains here:

> *But I speak this by permission, and not of commandment. For I would that all men were even as I myself. But every man hath his proper gift of God, one after this manner, and another after that. I say therefore to the unmarried and widows, It is good for them if they abide*

> *even as I. But if they cannot contain, let them marry: for it is better to marry than to burn.*
>
> 1 Corinthians 7:6–9

Paul was saying he had the gift to remain single, but not all people do, so it's best for them to get married.

Gays are wonderful people, and I love them, and you should love them, too, because God loves them. It is the practice of homosexuality He doesn't love. I pray that the homosexuals who read this chapter will want out of this deadly and destructive lifestyle after learning the truth behind homosexuality. I want to say to you, most of all, that God absolutely loves you, no matter how far you have fallen into sin. You may have done something horrible in the past because you were under the control of a diabolical, evil spirit inside of you. Sometimes you may wonder if God will ever forgive you. Yes, He will forgive you. However, you must pray for forgiveness for your sins and deliverance from this bondage of homosexuality and for salvation.

I want to invite you to pray this prayer:

> *Father God, I am a sinner, and I'm confused with who I am. I have struggled for years with my identity. I am not genuinely happy, and no matter what I try, I am still empty inside. Now I know what is missing, and that's you, Father God. Please forgive me for all my sins and come into my heart and save my soul from hell and deliver me from the evil spirits of homosexuality, as I denounce it and Satan himself and ask you to create in me a clean heart. And give me the strength and courage to obey and follow you, to live according to Your Holy Word. And I will serve*

> *You all the days of my life. I am tired of running from You, knowing I cannot hide from Your presence, for You are Almighty God, all-knowing, all-powerful, all-seeing, and I am but dust. From dust was I taken and to dust shall I return. I ask that You, save me right now, O Lord, and create in me a clean heart, God, and fill me with the precious gift of the Holy Spirit. Amen.*

Now that you have prayed a broken sinner's prayer and asked the Lord into your heart, you should be experiencing a peace upon you that surpasses all your understanding of the Holy Ghost, the Spirit of God Himself. I also want to encourage you to go and seek the Lord. Jeremiah 29:11–13 says:

> *For I know the thoughts that I think toward you, saith the LORD, thoughts of peace, and not of evil, to give you an expected end. Then shall ye call upon me, and ye shall go and pray unto me, and I will hearken unto you. And ye shall seek me, and find me, when ye shall search for me with all your heart.*

Be sure to find a strong and anointed Bible-teaching church that believes in the power of prayer and fasting and the Baptism of the Holy Ghost. The Bible says that there are some spirits that only leave you by prayer and fasting. Mark 9:28–29:

> *And when he was come into the house, his disciples asked him privately, Why could not we cast him out? And he said unto them, This kind can come forth by nothing, but by prayer and fasting.*

Also, never give up. First Timothy 6:12 says:

> *Fight the good fight of faith, lay hold on eternal life, whereunto thou art also called, and hast professed a good profession before many witnesses.*

Homosexuality will always be an abomination and unacceptable to God, no matter how man tries to approve of it. It is an act of evil, and any nation or people practicing it will bring God's inevitable judgment upon it. According to Psalm 9:17:

> *The wicked shall be turned into hell, and all the nations that forget God.*

It doesn't surprise me to see such rapid change in public opinion in favor of this movement, simply because God's Word says in the last days that it will be like Sodom and Gomorrah. Therefore, I want to say to the Church, be not dismayed, because there is a bright side to all of this. Christ, the Bridegroom, is soon to return for His bride, the Church. This is another sign that truly, we are living in the perilous times that the Lord speaks of in 2 Timothy 3:1–5:

> *This know also, that in the last days perilous times shall come. For men shall be lovers of their own selves, covetous, boasters, proud, blasphemers, disobedient to parents, unthankful, unholy, Without natural affection, trucebreakers, false accusers, incontinent, fierce, despisers of*

> *those that are good, Traitors, heady, highminded, lovers of pleasures more than lovers of God; Having a form of godliness, but denying the power thereof: from such turn away.*

Notice verse 3 says, "Without natural affection…" This means people being attracted to the same sex. There are some who think that God's ban on homosexuality was just an Old Testament law, which doesn't apply to us today. However, on the contrary, here are scriptures from the New Testament that clearly point out that it is not a natural behavior for men to have sex with men, and God is still against it. These are undeniable scriptures about homosexuals and those who rejected God and His Word, whose minds became reprobate, to the point they could not discern right from wrong. Also, these scriptures point out clearly what state the world will be in, in the last and evil days before Christ returns to take away the righteous.

> *Because that, when they knew God, they glorified him not as God, neither were thankful; but became vain in their imaginations, and their foolish heart was darkened. Professing themselves to be wise, they became fools, And changed the glory of the uncorruptible God into an image made like to corruptible man, and to birds, and fourfooted beasts, and creeping things. Wherefore God also gave them up to uncleanness through the lusts of their own hearts, to dishonour their own bodies between themselves: Who changed the truth of God into a lie, and worshipped and served the creature more than the Creator, who is blessed for ever. Amen. For this cause God gave them up unto vile affections: for even their women did change the natural*

> use into that which is against nature: And likewise also the men, leaving the natural use of the woman, burned in their lust one toward another; men with men working that which is unseemly, and receiving in themselves that recompence of their error which was meet. And even as they did not like to retain God in their knowledge, God gave them over to a reprobate mind, to do those things which are not convenient; Being filled with all unrighteousness, fornication, wickedness, covetousness, maliciousness; full of envy, murder, debate, deceit, malignity; whisperers, Backbiters, haters of God, despiteful, proud, boasters, inventors of evil things, disobedient to parents, Without understanding, covenantbreakers, without natural affection, implacable, unmerciful: Who knowing the judgment of God, that they which commit such things are worthy of death, not only do the same, but have pleasure in them that do them.
>
> Romans 1:21–32

This is one of the scriptures that points out some of the evil things that will take place on the earth in last and evil days before Christ returns to take away the righteous people.

I have heard some say that other countries allow same-sex marriages, so why shouldn't the United States? And my response is this: when I was a kid, I would ask my mom if I could do this or that, but as a caring mother knowing it was not in my best interest, she would say no. And, of course, I would say, "But all the other kids are doing it."

She would reply with something like, "If all your friends jumped off a cliff into an icy river, would you?"

So, I say to you, just because other countries are allowing it does not mean America should. We are not another country. We are America, which is supposed to be a God-fearing nation, "the land of the free and the home of the brave," and yet we are slowly drifting away from God and His Holy Righteous Word, the Bible.

In conclusion:

Homosexuality. How does God feel about it? God hates the practice of it but loves the people. Just for the record, homosexuality is not my fight. According to God's Word, no one can stop the homosexual movement because the Word of God has declared the end time corruption of men's hearts and that the homosexuality movement is unstoppable; it will increase as it were in the days of Sodom and Gomorrah.

I believe it is important to inform the LGBTQ community that the rainbow you so proudly display internationally was originally designed by God. The people were so wicked in the days of Noah that God instructed Noah, the only righteous man during those days, to build an ark for him and his family to escape the destruction of the flood. Therefore, God caused it to rain for forty days and forty nights after He destroyed all living things, man, and animals in the flood. He made a covenant or an (agreement) with mankind and His creation that He will never destroy the world again by water. So, God made a rainbow in the sky as a symbol of His covenant so, whenever you see a rainbow in the sky, that's what it represents. Please read the scripture below that explains the origin of the rainbow:

> *And God spake unto Noah, and to his sons with him, saying, And I, behold, I establish my covenant with you, and with your seed after you; And with every living creature that is with you, of the fowl, of the cattle, and of*

every beast of the earth with you; from all that go out of the ark, to every beast of the earth. And I will establish my covenant with you; neither shall all flesh be cut off any more by the waters of a flood; neither shall there any more be a flood to destroy the earth. And God said, This is the token of the covenant which I make between me and you and every living creature that is with you, for perpetual generations: I do set my bow in the cloud, and it shall be for a token of a covenant between me and the earth. And it shall come to pass, when I bring a cloud over the earth, that the bow shall be seen in the cloud: And I will remember my covenant, which is between me and you and every living creature of all flesh; and the waters shall no more become a flood to destroy all flesh. And the bow shall be in the cloud; and I will look upon it, that I may remember the everlasting covenant between God and every living creature of all flesh that is upon the earth. And God said unto Noah, This is the token of the covenant, which I have established between me and all flesh that is upon the earth.

Genesis 9:8–17

Let it be known that you are using the rainbow and its colors for your own personal agenda and not what God intended it to represent. Keep in mind that God says He will not destroy the world by flood again because of man's wicked behavior, but He also says He will destroy the world by fire next time, and it reads:

But the day of the Lord will come as a thief in the night; in the which the heavens shall pass away with a great noise,

> *and the elements shall melt with fervent heat, the earth also and the works that are therein shall be burned up.*
>
> 2 Peter 3:10

Also read:

> *For if God spared not the angels that sinned, but cast them down to hell, and delivered them into chains of darkness, to be reserved unto judgment; And spared not the old world, but saved Noah the eighth person, a preacher of righteousness, bringing in the flood upon the world of the ungodly; And turning the cities of Sodom and Gomorrha into ashes condemned them with an overthrow, making them an ensample unto those that after should live ungodly; And delivered just Lot, vexed with the filthy conversation of the wicked.*
>
> 2 Peter 2:4–7

Often, we hear about the wrath of God and not His loving side. By character, God is loving, kind, gracious, compassionate, merciful, just, holy, wise, forgiving, lone suffering, slow to anger, faithful, and more. In these two scriptures, we find the beauty of God's loving, caring nature in 2 Peter 3:9.

> *The Lord is not slack concerning his promise, as some men count slackness; but is longsuffering to us-ward, not willing that any should perish, but that all should come to repentance.*

For God so loved the world, that he gave his only begotten Son, that whosoever believeth in him should not perish, but have everlasting life.

John 3:16

The rainbow should be a reminder to you to repent of sin, not to celebrate sin; So, please answer the call of God, and repent and be baptized in the name of our Lord and Savior Jesus Christ for the remission of sin and receive the gift of the Holy Ghost and live holy and you shall be saved.

My position is that the government should not be in the business of promoting laws to facilitate the wickedness of sodomy, known as homosexuality. I ask the African American community to please read chapter 6 on Politics and learn more about the anti-God agenda of the Democrat Party; perhaps, this may be your wake-up call to stop voting for them.

Whether you know it or not, you cannot run as a Democrat candidate and openly oppose homosexuality, same-sex marriage, and abortion because this is part of the loose, immoral, liberal Democrat Party agenda—which embraces the old "live and let live," do whatever you desire to do mindset, regardless of what God says. They say, just as long as you vote for me, I will support your ungodly ways. My job is to warn you, and I believe with the help of God Almighty, I have done that well. As a sign from heaven that God is against the practice and perversion of sodomy in the U.S. Armed Forces, He will allow a conflict between the bear and the eagle, and the bear shall wound the eagle.

The bright side is that God chastises (corrects) those whom He loves.

For whom the Lord loveth he chasteneth, and scourgeth every son whom he receiveth.

Hebrews 12:6

Sincerely, written with love and concern for you.

CHAPTER TWO
ABORTION

WHAT IS ABORTION?

It is a procedure the government allows doctors to perform that murders innocent, unborn babies. Basically, it is human sacrifice and a license to kill for monetary gain and convenience for the mother-to-be. All these doctors and clinic assistants should be arrested and tried for crimes against humanity. It is insane for *us, the people,* to sit back and allow something like this to happen on our watch. It's a shame and unacceptable. Making abortion illegal is not bad as people might think; for those who do not know, there are thirty-seven countries where abortion is illegal except in the case of saving the life of the mother. The reason we have such a big push back to keep abortion legal is because in America, we use this loophole in the law for convenience to put down the baby for whatever reasons, just for the mother's convenience. So sad.

Roe vs. Wade must be overturned so that the blood of the innocent will not be on our hands. We, the people, have the power, not our government. We put them in office. Let us bind together and put an end to this madness.

In 1973, in a landmark decision, the U.S. Supreme Court decided on the issue of abortion. The court ruled 7–2 that a right to privacy under the due process clause of the Fourteenth Amendment should be extended to a woman choosing to have an abortion.

In this case, the justices gave their own interpretation of the Fourteenth Amendment clause. The Fourteenth Amendment to the Constitution was ratified on July 9, 1868.

It granted citizenship to "all persons born or naturalized in the United States," which included former slaves who were recently freed. This Amendment was later extended to protect the privacy rights of individuals. Once this happened, no one could invade or interfere with his or her privacy, family, home, or correspondence so as not to attack his or her honor and reputation.

It goes on to say in the Fourteenth Amendment, Section 1:

"All persons born or naturalized in the United States, and subject to the jurisdiction thereof, are citizens of the United States and of the state wherein they reside. No state shall make or enforce any law which shall abridge the privileges or immunities of citizens of the United States; nor shall any state deprive any person of life, liberty, or property, without due process of law; nor deny to any person within its jurisdiction the equal protection of the laws." This amendment does not support prochoice, but on the contrary, it does support pro-life in the clause "equal protection of the laws."

Once again, we find ourselves back at the Supreme Court waging spiritual war to overturn *Roe vs. Wade* in the Senate Bill 8 of the Texas Abortion Law.

During the hearings, one Supreme Court Justice said the word fetus is not in the Constitution. I mean, really? Do you need to literally see the word fetus to draw a reasonable and common-sense conclusion that abortion is unconstitutional? The word *fetus* does not have to be spelled out in the Constitution. Furthermore, the Founding Fathers who wrote the constitution did not imagine that society would end up in such dark places, to the point where they needed to spell out specific things such as abortion issues in the constitution. In the Fourteenth Amendment, Section 1, the last paragraph states, "nor deny to any person within his jurisdiction the equal protection of the laws." The word person is a fetus; undeniable, the fetus is a person; please do not complicate it. I would like to encourage the justices not to feel you need to recuse yourself; recusal is not an option and the fight to protect precious, helpless, unborn souls is inexcusable. What you should understand and remember is you, as a conservative, are all types of Esther, and the liberals are types of Haman who seek to increase the genocidal atrocity of the unborn, and God has put you in the position that you are in, for such a time as this. For those who do not know the story, Esther, who was Jewish, married an Old Testament king, and Haman was chief officer second in command to the king, who hated the Jews and sought to destroy them. However, Esther devised a plan and stopped the ethnic cleansing plot, and saved all the Jews during that time.

How does granting a woman permission to have an abortion have anything to do with the original privacy law? Abortion is not a private matter; it is murder.

To obtain a better understanding of what this law is about, read the following examples.

Example #1: Let's say a married female Chief Executive Officer goes on a business trip overseas, accompanied by a male colleague. After three days of business, they have a casual dinner together. On the last night, after a few drinks, they end up in bed together. Several weeks later, after returning to the States, she realizes she is pregnant. She fears losing her family, husband, big home, and career, so she decides to have an abortion. Does this mean she should have the right to choose? *No!* This is nothing but human sacrifice camouflaged in the name of abortion. So, she murders the baby to save her way of life. The baby is put to death because of her mistake in the name of a right to choose. Hmm…

Example #2: This time, I will use a prominent family. They have a daughter that they thought was a little angel. There are many weekends she stays out late, and they think she is spending time with her girlfriend. But instead, she is with her boyfriend. You guessed it right; she ends up getting pregnant. What's next? The parents sit her down and instruct her to have an abortion. Why? The family's name is at stake, and besides that, this boy who got her pregnant is from the wrong side of the town, and the girl must remember her educational goals. She was accepted at Yale University. So, they sacrifice the baby in the name of pride and education.

Finally, *Example #3:* There is a young, single, minority woman who already has three children. She gets pregnant again due to her promiscuous behavior. She goes to the local Planned Parenthood facility for so-called prenatal care and counseling, where they talk her into having an abortion by suppressing the truth about the procedure. They tell her it is not a real baby anyway, but mere tissue mass, even though she's in her 23rd week of gestation, which is a known fact for viability, which means the baby has developed enough to live outside his mother's womb. After convincing her to have the abortion, she now feels her burden is lifted from the responsibility of raising another child. But on the contrary, and unknowingly to her, she will soon be weighed down with the burden of guilt. They never inform the mother-to-be that abortions hurt not just physically but emotionally, mentally, and spiritually. Sometimes a woman who receives an abortion carries this heavy, guilty burden around for the rest of her life. What a price to pay! The burden of committing murder is so heavy that only God can lift it. The Sixth Commandment says in Exodus 20:13, *"Thou shalt not kill."*

As the price of sin keeps adding up, taxpayers are out of more money. Most importantly, an innocent life has been senselessly taken, leaving the parasite Planned Parenthood with fatter pockets. Do not be mistaken; these con artists are good at what they do. They must be in order to get more federal funding that comes from the taxpayers. Yes, you heard me right. We, as Christians, are financing this atrocity. One of the most hidden secrets of Planned Parenthood is that they harvest body parts from aborted babies and sell them for profit. How sick is that? This mean-spirited, well-financed fat-killing machine known as Planned Parenthood must be defunded as soon as possible. Something must be done about this new form of genocide. Just how did we get here? Why don't we start from the beginning with *Roe vs. Wade*?

Once there was a pregnant single woman by the name of Norma L. McCorvey. In 1969, she became pregnant with her third child. She returned to Dallas, where her friends advised her to assert falsely that she had been raped to obtain a legal abortion. She did so with the understanding that Texas law allows abortions in cases of rape and incest. Her plot did not work because there was no report made to the police regarding a rape incident.

She attempted to obtain an illegal abortion but found the unauthorized site closed by the police. Eventually, she was referred to attorneys, but—thank God—McCorvey would give birth before the case was decided. Norma never had an abortion. She gave her baby up for adoption. For several years, Norma was silent about her role as Jane Roe. In the 1980s, she became involved in the abortion movement, making public appearances in support of abortion. In 1992, she began to work at an abortion clinic, having no actual experience with abortion until that point. In a statement at the time, she wrote, "Becoming even more emotionally confused and conflicted between what my conscience knows to be evil, but the need for money was telling me it was okay."

Norma was working at a clinic in Dallas in 1995. A pro-life group moved into the same building, and over time, she became friends with them. The rest is history; after conversion, she dedicated herself to the pro-life movement and even started her own ministry. Her story reminds me of the old "Amazing Grace" lyrics: "I once was lost, but now am found; was blind, but now I see."

Norma repented and put herself on the right side of history by experiencing God's saving grace. That goes to show that it's never too late. God can turn the hardest hearts around.

Norma McCorvey's heart became more convinced that the unborn, aborted baby wasn't just a blob or mass of tissue. If you are not convinced yet, I would like for you to visit https://www.priestsforlife.org/images/abortion-images-galleries.aspx

Warning: The pictures on this website are very graphic and may not be suitable for viewing by young children. However, I believe after you view these aborted images of these precious little souls, you should have a complete change of heart; if you have a pure heart and a white soul, it will bring you to tears once you view them.

I've got to tell you that no matter how many times I see these pictures, they still break my heart and oftentimes move me to tears. Because these pictures cut right through my heart, it is hard to imagine that anyone would not be moved by them. Yes, what you are seeing are real human beings—baby's body parts and limbs—that were pulled apart during the extraction from the warmth and safety of mother's womb; for whatever reason, the mother cut her precious child's life short. These are children that America is slaughtering every day.

What one must understand is that, during pregnancy, an embryo develops inside the woman's uterus. An embryo is a developing offspring during the first eight weeks after conception.

The scientific community has been known to use the term *fetus* until birth. This growth is divided into three periods called trimesters. These trimesters are described as high-risk periods of advanced growth and fetal viability until the point when life can be sustained outside the uterus.

If you view this as nothing more than a mass of tissue at any point, you are looking at it the wrong way. To keep a clear understanding, one must see it as life from the moment of conception because that's how God sees it. If you don't, then Satan can mislead you. Here's a U.S. abortion statistic: since *Roe vs. Wade*—from 1973 to 2021, approximately sixty-two million babies have been aborted. God only knows how many Albert Einsteins, Wright Brothers, Dr. Martin Luther Kings, and Thomas Edisons, even heroes of faith like Moses, Jeremiah, and Josiah, have been aborted since *Roe vs. Wade*.

So, why do women have abortions?

Some say having a baby would interfere with work, school, or other things. Some have thoughts such as:

- "I don't want to be a single parent or have relationship problems with my husband or partner."
- "A baby does not fit into my current education or career plans."
- "I became pregnant as a result of being raped or was victimized by incest."

Most reasons for abortions are centered on the needs of mothers' and fathers' lame excuses rather than the baby's right to live.

For those who believe in abortion, their number one defense is no one should have the right to tell me what I can and cannot do with my body, and I must say you are right; no one should try to tell you what to do with your body. However, to a certain extent, the government should regulate the action you perform with your body, and they do, such as preventing you from selling your body in the form of prostitution or from putting illegal drugs in your body, causing bodily harm to you and potentially other people. On the other hand, if you want to tattoo your whole body like a lizard or permanently tattoo your face as a clown face, you have the right to do so because it is your body, even though I would not recommend doing such a thing. On the contrary, in the case of abortion, we are not trying to tell you what you can and can't do with your body; we are telling you, you do not have the right to take a life just because you are carrying it in your God-given womb. Only God has the right, and God, only to decide which baby should live or die, which baby should be born blind, lame, deaf, mute, or mentally challenged; I call them God's little earthly angels. There should be no exception for abortion, except for the rare case of an ectopic pregnancy, also called extrauterine pregnancy, when a fertilized egg grows outside a woman's uterus somewhere else in her abdomen. It can cause life-threatening bleeding and needs medical care right away. Other than this rare case, you should let the Lord's will be done, not your will. By the way, I would like to know who made you judge, jury, and executioner to decide to take a precious baby's life?

Some say, "I cannot afford to have another baby"; what about years ago, when people had large families, sometimes as many as twelve children, during the Depression? They somehow still raised their families. Why can't you? With so many available programs to help aid you, such as adoption agencies, ministries, and pro-life agencies, there is no excuse for abortion.

I pray that God will open your eyes and convince you that unborn babies are real. Even our law points to the fact that an unborn baby is real. For example, if a man crashes into a pregnant woman's car while driving under the influence and kills both the woman and the unborn child, he will be charged with double vehicular homicide. So why is it murder in this case and not in the case of abortion? What a contradiction of the law and hypocrisy.

Please visit *lyna.org* or *www.loveyourneighboramerica.org* and become a LYNA partner. We are believing God to assemble a small army of believers by 2025 that will stand together to send a strong message to America and Washington that we want godly leaders that will protect the unborn. We are tired of these flip-floppers and poll-watchers who would sell their souls to get elected (or re-elected). I plead with our current president Joe Biden to do the right thing by having the courage to denounce abortion because you know better; your faith has taught you for years that abortion is a horrible injustice. Mr. President, it is not too late to get on the right side of God and history and become a pro-life president who helped save the lives of innocent unborn babies, regardless of how your constituents and colleagues feel.

For those who are still in doubt, I ask you to please be open-minded and sensitive to the Holy Spirit, and God will show you the truth. If God opened the eyes of the woman who helped start it all, I am sure He can open your eyes also. After this last point, I will rest my case.

Under our law, if one person has been accused by another and convicted of a crime and sent to prison based on that testimony, and their accuser later recants his statement (perhaps by admitting to lying under oath) or is proven wrong, the accused is released. The accused is acquitted immediately because the accuser admitted he lied. In *Roe vs. Wade,* we have the accuser, the late Norma L. McCorvey, who initially didn't think much of it, so she felt it was okay to have an abortion. Since then, she has realized she was wrong, and former abortionist doctors have admitted they were wrong and that the babies are real, living human beings in the mother's womb. Therefore, the baby should be recognized as a human being and freed from the death penalty of abortion. Why won't the Supreme Court philosophically acquit the babies by banning abortion? But instead, the court is breaking a law referred to as *double jeopardy.* The Fifth Amendment in the U.S. Constitution prohibits anyone from being prosecuted twice for the same charges.

The charge made by the accuser's former abortion doctors that the fetus is not a real baby has been recanted. Their story testified and proved that the fetus is life inside the mother's womb. I would like to know why a defenseless baby can be charged with the notion that he is not a real human. Guess what, people? The baby is a living human being inside the mother's womb, whether you believe it or not. There is a life inside a woman's uterus from the time of conception when that one little Olympic champion swimmer finishes his course and penetrates the ovum. The life cycle has begun. The opinions regarding when consciousness and the ability to feel pain starts and viability are irrelevant. God's creation has begun. He wants the mother to protect this precious life from the first day until her ninth month.

Even nature itself teaches us when life begins. Take a plant seed, for example; when it's planted in the ground, the soil becomes the fertilizer, which starts the germination process. From there, the plant starts to emerge from the seed out of the ground. Now when the plant, which is life itself, gets proper light, water, warmth, and minerals, it germinates faster. But without these necessities, it won't survive once the process of life is underway. The same is true as it relates to the embryo. In this case, life has begun, and therefore the embryo needs the mother's womb to nourish the life in her until birth.

If the plant is disturbed, stepped on, or starved of nutrients, it will die. For something to die, it first must be alive. So, when the plant dies, there is no tree, and if there is no tree, there is no fruit. So it is with human life; if a nation continues to kill the fetus—which is human—there will be fewer babies; fewer babies, lower population, and lower population equal a weak, dying out, old nation. Even Russia has found this to be true. I found an article saying that Russia is considering banning abortion, realizing the long-term effects it wreaks on the population. The article stated, "Last month, Russian President Vladimir Putin signed a law banning abortion advertising." Some members of the *Duma*, the Russian state assembly, are talking about going even further and banning the procedure itself. The Russian Orthodox Church, whose numbers are swelling with converts, is weighing in as well. One Orthodox prelate called abortion "a mutiny against God."

This is an amazing turnabout in a country that has long been known for its tragically high abortion rate. Until recently, the average woman in Russia could expect to have seven abortions over her lifetime. Here again, we find Russia's moral view is clearer and wiser than that of the U.S. when it comes to abortion.

I must say, this is one of the most profound statements I have heard describing abortion: "a mutiny against God." I don't know who this Orthodox prelate is, but I'd certainly like to say, "God bless you." And if he doesn't mind, I am going to use this phrase every chance I get in the public arena because it is so precise. A mutiny occurs when a group of people or sailors refuse to obey orders and rise up to take control away from the person in charge. Now, isn't that what we are seeing with the abortion issue? Who's in command? God, right? Who is refusing to obey? Man (liberals). What order are they refusing to obey, which was given by the true Commander in Chief? "Thou shall not kill."

I mean, come on, America. Please don't allow Satan to deceive you on this issue. As I'm writing this, I'm trying to keep my composure. Sometimes it's hard to hold back because it's so disturbing to me how we allow this to continue. I truly believe that the Spirit of God is speaking through me to move you to act on behalf of the powerless, innocent unborn babies. To become a voice for those who cannot speak for themselves. But certainly, they can feel the pain that's afflicted upon them by money-hungry, greedy abortionist doctors whose hearts have been hardened by Satan.

I leave you with one scripture showing that life in God's eyes starts long before conception. If you cannot believe God, whom can you believe?

> *Then the word of the LORD came unto me, saying, Before I formed thee in the belly I knew thee; and before thou camest forth out of the womb I sanctified thee, and I ordained thee a prophet unto the nations.*
>
> Jeremiah 1:4–5

What God is saying to Jeremiah is that He knew him even before he existed, and He was preparing him for His work when he was a fetus in his mother's womb. I can't make it any plainer than life starts at conception. If you can't believe God, who else will you believe? I ask you to please pray for me as I seek to help put an end to this spiritual war of abortion in America. With God's help, together, we can put an end to this barbaric, savage, vicious, wicked, and heinous crime that's carried out every day in a so-called Christian nation. I would like to know where the Christians are when God needs us the most. I thank God for Pope Francis, for his clear and strong opposition to the evilness of abortion, and the Catholic Church that's on the front line in the war on sanctity of life. How about you? Are you too occupied with your own affairs and the cares of this life? Have you forgotten why we are here, that we are to be a light to the world? Will you please stand with me and help put an end to abortion on our watch?

In Conclusion:

Abortion. How does God feel about abortion? It sheds the blood of precious, innocent, little souls; the procedure is barbaric at the highest level, and it is an act of evil.

Now, just for the record, this is my fight. Together we can and must put an end to this madness called abortion that plagues and curses our country.

In the words of a forgotten pioneer, William Tyndale, whose prayer was that God would open the eyes of the King of England as Tyndale was strangled to death and burned at the stake for translating the Bible from Greek to English which was illegal to do in the early 15th century.

"In August 1536, he was condemned; on this day, October 6, 1536, he was strangled and his body burned at the stake. His last prayer was, 'Lord, open the King of England's eyes.'"

The prayer was answered in part when three years later, in 1539, Henry VIII required every parish church in England to make a copy of the English Bible available to its parishioners. The point is, Tyndale was a man of passion, conviction, and, above all, courage to stand up for what he knew was right, which compelled him to produce the world's first translation of the Bible from Greek to English so that peasants and average people would be able to read the Holy Bible for themselves, and not having to solely rely on the priest to read it to them. My prayer is that God opens the eyes of the Supreme Court and the leaders of this great nation that they may see abortion as wrong and give them the courage to put an end to this atrocity against the unborn on their watch. Also, I pray that God opens the eyes of the minority communities to see that abortion clinics target them the most with their genocidal program called Planned Parenthood, and tragically, the left-wing liberals are too blind to see that abortion is wrong. The ungodly practice of abortion reminds me of the title of Harper Lee's 1960 classic, *To Kill a Mockingbird*. Even though the meaning of the title remains unclear, many readers have concluded that it speaks of the innocence of the mockingbird. The story unfolds when the small-town Alabama Black man Tom Robinson—well-known as a harmless, friendly, submissive person—is accused of raping a poor White woman named Mayella Ewell. When she hires him to come into her home to do some manual labor, she makes a sexual advance on him, which he refuses. As the case goes to trial with an all-White, racist jury, Tom, the falsely accused Black man, has a well-known lawyer named Atticus, who is known for defending poor Black people. Still, they lose the case, and Tom is sentenced to death. After seeing so many innocent, harmless defendants convicted and sent to death row, Atticus shares a metaphor with his young daughter, Scout, saying, "It's a sin to kill a mockingbird." Toward the story's end, Scout defends the actions of Boo Radley, her heroic, artistic neighbor, who stabs and kills her evil neighbor Bob Ewell, the alleged rape victim's father, when he tries to assault her and her brother. Scout feels that Boo is a mentally challenged, innocent soul who does not deserve to be tried for murder and put to death for killing evil Bob Ewell and thus saving her life. Thereafter, she reminds her father, Atticus the lawyer, that "it's a sin to kill a mockingbird," apparently influencing Atticus and the town's sheriff to secretly agree not to press charges against Boo.

So, what is it about mockingbirds—those harmless, innocent, happy, charming, singing little birds? They show up in your backyard to greet you with cheerful songs, flitting and fluttering with dancing movements that will surely intrigue you and brighten your day. So, it would be a sin for someone to go out back and shoot such a harmless little bird. Likewise, I remind you again that it's a sin to kill an innocent, harmless, defenseless, unborn, precious baby, whom God has given to you to bring you joy and gladness, and whom God has given a unique purpose in this world.

Written with the deepest sadness.

As a sign from heaven that God is against the sin of human sacrifice known as abortion, He will allow a conflict between the bear and the eagle, and the bear shall wound the eagle.

Please pray for me, Apostle R. S. Porter, that I may help put an end to abortion with the help of The Almighty God. God bless you, and thank you so much for your support.

CHAPTER THREE
CRIME

Crime is no stranger to civilization; it's been around since the beginning of mankind. When you search the Holy Scriptures, you will find that the very first crime was committed shortly after God made man. Here is an account of the incident.

Cain Murders Abel

And Cain talked with Abel his brother: and it came to pass, when they were in the field, that Cain rose up against Abel his brother, and slew him. And the LORD said unto Cain, Where is Abel thy brother? And he said, I know not: Am I my brother's keeper? And he said, What hast thou done? the voice of thy brother's blood crieth unto me from the ground. And now art thou cursed from the earth, which hath opened her mouth to receive thy brother's blood from thy hand; When thou tillest the ground, it shall not henceforth yield unto thee her strength; a fugitive and a vagabond shalt thou be in the earth. And Cain said unto the LORD, My punishment is greater than I can bear. Behold, thou hast driven me out this day from the face of the earth; and from thy face shall I be hid; and I shall be a fugitive and a vagabond in the earth; and it shall come to pass, that every one that findeth me shall slay me. And the LORD said unto him, Therefore whosoever slayeth Cain, vengeance shall be taken

> on him sevenfold. And the LORD set a mark upon Cain, lest any finding him should kill him.
>
> Genesis 4:8–15

Here we see a man named Cain who committed the first murder in the world when he killed his brother, Abel. Why? We will get to that question a little later. There are many types of crimes; here is an alphabetical list of common crimes:

- Arson
- Aggravated Assault / Battery
- Attempt
- Bribery
- Burglary
- Child Abandonment
- Child Abuse
- Child Pornography
- Computer Crime
- Conspiracy
- Credit / Debit Card Fraud
- Criminal Contempt of Court
- Cyber Bullying
- Disorderly Conduct
- Disturbing the Peace
- Domestic Violence
- Drug Manufacturing and Cultivation
- Drug Possession
- Drug Trafficking / Distribution
- DUI / DWI
- Embezzlement
- Extortion

- Forgery
- Fraud
- Harassment
- Hate Crimes
- Homicide
- Indecent Exposure
- Identity Theft
- Insurance Fraud
- Kidnapping
- Manslaughter: Involuntary
- Manslaughter: Voluntary
- Medical Marijuana
- MIP: A Minor in Possession
- Money Laundering
- Murder: First-degree
- Murder: Second-degree
- Open Container Law
- Perjury
- Probation Violation
- Prostitution
- Public Intoxication
- Pyramid Schemes
- Racketeering / RICO
- Rape
- Robbery
- Securities Fraud
- Sexual Assault
- Shoplifting
- Solicitation
- Stalking

- Statutory Rape
- Tax Evasion / Fraud
- Telemarketing Fraud
- Theft/Larceny
- Vandalism
- White Collar Crimes
- Wire Fraud

The top three most horrible crimes, in my opinion, are murder, child molestation, and rape. Child molestation is a big no-no. When it comes to innocent children, most people have zero tolerance and little to no mercy for pedophiles, who are monsters that prey on the innocence of little kids. But as a Christian, one must still find a way to exercise forgiveness and pray that God has mercy on their souls. Sex offenders come in all forms and disguises, especially in the wake of the #METOO movement, where we have seen many women are coming out seeking help and healing from many years of sexual abuse and misconduct by unsuspected men. We need to take this opportunity to empower the woman from being a victim to a victor and turn the table from shame on the victims to shamefulness on the predators who prey on helpless women. Also, we need to take a stand against organized sex trafficking crimes, where women are sold as sex slaves at an alarming rate. And even murderers should be forgiven. Some murderers are given the death penalty. I, however, am 100% against capital punishment because not everyone the state puts to death will be guilty. Therefore, this equates to human sacrifice as a means of deterring crime. There is no evidence that state executions deter crime, and there is evidence that the government has executed innocent people. The question is, who is willing to take responsibility and answer to God for murdering the innocent along with the guilty?

Why do people commit crimes? We can turn to crime analysts, who examine patterns and trends in crime and disorder. However, in the end, there are several reasons people commit crimes. To me, the most obvious reasons why people commit crimes are:
1. Not genuinely saved and having no fear of God.
2. Sensing a lack of opportunity, known as despair.
3. Having an evil heart, which leads to greed and jealousy.

Reason 1: A non-believer and people who have no fear of God will do just about anything for their own profits and gain, unlike a Christian who, fearing God, will not take advantage of someone for self-gain. The scripture says in Luke 6:31,

> *And as ye would that men should do to you, do ye also to them likewise.*

In addition, Saint Mark offers another account of how a believer should act:

> *And one of the scribes came, and having heard them reasoning together, and perceiving that he had answered them well, asked him, Which is the first commandment of all? And Jesus answered him, The first of all the commandments is, Hear, O Israel; The Lord our God is one Lord: And thou shalt love the Lord thy God with all thy heart, and with all thy soul, and with all thy mind, and with all thy strength: this is the first commandment. And the second is like, namely this, Thou shalt love thy neigh-*

bour as thyself. There is none other commandment greater than these.

Mark 12:28–31

So, to put it simply, if you are saved, love God, and love your neighbor as thyself, you should not commit crimes. Crimes are mostly something that unsaved non-believers will do.

Reason 2: Lack of opportunity, which leads to feelings of despair, hopelessness, and desperation. When folks become desperate, they will do whatever it takes to survive. Yes, that includes stealing and all sorts of crimes. But does that make it right to break the law? No. However, if a person commits a crime out of desperation, should not that person be shown mercy?

Here's a good example. Let's say the country's economy collapses, and we fall into economic depression, in which the gross domestic product hits rock bottom, and the unemployment rate goes up to thirty percent. Keep in mind the record high occurred in 1932 when it hit twenty-three percent. Imagine a man named Bob, who has five children and who has lost his job at a local lumber mill that has gone out of business. Bob cannot find work, and the kids haven't eaten in a week.

Three miles down an old country road, there is a farmer known as Grumpy Farmer Jack, who's not known for his generosity and who is rather mean-spirited. He has posted *"No Trespassing"* signs around his cornfield and apple orchard, and he would not give Bob or anyone else the time of day. Now Bob is in despair due to a lack of opportunity. So, what should he do? There is no public assistance, and the kids are so hungry they can't even fall asleep. Now put yourself in Bob's shoes. What would you do? I believe nine out of ten people would go down to Farmer Jack's farm at night and take the liberty of gathering up a bushel of corn and some apples to feed his family. Does that make him a bad guy or an evil person? No. If he gets caught, should mercy be shown? Yes, because he was a man who was forced to use what we all have instilled in us: an instinctive will to survive. Now this crime was not committed out of greed but survival due to the lack of opportunities.

You will find in the book of Proverbs 6:30–31:

> *Men do not despise a thief, if he steal to satisfy his soul when he is hungry; But if he be found, he shall restore sevenfold; he shall give all the substance of his house.*

Notice that even though Bob's actions seem justifiable, they still would not go unpunished. In the end, he must make restitution. What did we learn from this example? We have learned that a man will do what a man must do in order to survive, even if it means committing a crime. The other lesson we have learned is no crime is justifiable. However, the reality of it all is that many crimes are committed because of a lack of opportunity, which leads to desperation to obtain the fundamental needs of life.

Reason 3: Remember when I asked you earlier in the chapter why did Cain commit the first murder in the world, the man who killed his own brother Abel? Ok, we can find our answer in our third reason for crime. People commit crimes because of an evil heart, greed, and jealousy; the scripture below points it out.

> *For this is the message that ye heard from the beginning, that we should love one another. Not as Cain, who was of that wicked one, and slew his brother. And wherefore slew he him? Because his own works were evil, and his brother's righteous.*
>
> 1 John 3:11–12

Most crimes are committed because of man's evil heart and greed. Cain was the world's first murderer. His punishment for his thuggish ways was that God made him a fugitive and a vagabond, meaning that he was cast out of the community, only to wander from place to place without a home or job. So, I say to the thug, if you act like a thug, we are going to treat you like one.

Let's probe deeper into crime in America. The crime rate in the Inner City is unimaginable, especially in Detroit, Baltimore, Oakland, and Milwaukee.

There could come a time when no one is safe; some people have a mentality like, I do not care as long as it's not in my neighborhood. The reality is that crime affects about everybody, whether we're talking higher premiums for insurance due to grand theft auto, higher condominium fees for extra security, or higher retail costs.

There is no stereotyping in the retail business; a thief has no one particular color. There is a little bit of everybody committing theft—red, yellow, black, white, young, and old. If you saw someone stealing in a retail store, would you turn the other way and mind your own business, as they say, or would you secretly report it to the manager? If you say nothing, you are doing yourself a disservice because you'll soon be the one paying for it through an increase in prices. Theft and fraud cost retailers $62 billion in 2020, up from $51 billion the previous year, according to a

National Retail Federation survey. These losses—which retailers refer to as shrink—represented about 1.6% of sales last year, up from 1.4% the previous year. The survey analyzed theft incidents from 118 of the largest U.S. retail chains. It was reported that an average family of four would spend more than $443 per year on higher prices due to retail crimes. Whether you accept it or not, crime in America is on the rise, especially in wake of the smash and grab retail crimes. So, are you a complainer, or are you a solution to the problem?

There are two more types of crimes I would like to mention. The first is black-on-black crime, which has reached epidemic levels and must stop. One idea on how to end it is through tough love—with emphasis on love—even if it means a nationwide workforce program that reaches out to all the gang members and repeat offenders on the streets who want help. This program would target those who desire change in their lives through faith-based concepts and boot camp discipline training. They would be able to learn a trade and eventually find a job and become law-abiding, taxpaying citizens with incentives to become homeowners. Those who do not desire to adapt to mainstream society should be kept off the streets for their safety and the public's, while we continue to work with them toward rehabilitation.

Most inner-city crimes stem from drug sales, gangs, or a lack of opportunity. In the case of the drug epidemic problem, they are not the main culprits; but instead, they are mere pawns in a much larger game. Now, if you only focus on the African American kids, everyone knows that these young people do not have the resources to bankroll large drug operations, such as manufacturing it in labs or having access to necessary transportation to move large quantities across international borders. But guess who takes the fall for most of the drug trafficking? You guessed it right, the young African American kid who has no father figure to help guide him in life. This kid is not a thug; he became a sacrificed pawn in the drug game. They are simply carriers, the hands and feet of the real thugs who stand at the head of the operation. I am not defending the actions of these young kids, but the fact is they really have no idea of the seriousness of street crime that can potentially destroy their lives; all they see is the lifestyle of their role models they look up to, which doesn't do them any good.

The solution is to cut off the head of the snake (The Kingpin) and allow the body to die (The Pawn). Right now, the hands and feet become the scapegoats who land in prison and receive excessive time that does not fit the crime. Needless to say, the head gets away and finds new hands and feet to use as little pawns in their criminal empires.

While I respect Mrs. Hillary R. Clinton for her service to our great nation, at the same time, I do not agree with some of her political views, so I will respectfully agree to disagree. Mrs. Clinton made a statement back in 1996 where she called young Black youth *superpredators*; the superpredators line comes from a 1996 speech in New Hampshire, where Clinton spoke in support of the 1994 Violent Crime Control and Law Enforcement Act, which her husband, former President Bill Clinton, had signed into law.

"We're making some progress," Clinton said. "Much of it is related to the initiative called 'community policing.' Because we have finally gotten more police officers on the street. That was one of the goals that the president had when he pushed the crime bill that was passed in 1994. They are not just gangs of kids anymore. They are often the kinds of kids that are called 'superpredators.'

No conscience, no empathy. We can talk about why they ended up that way, but first, we have to bring them to heel."

It was the largest crime bill passed in the history of the country; the Violent Crime Control and Law Enforcement Act contributed to an already mass incarceration of Black and Brown men, which was basically rounding up minorities and sending them off to prison with little to no hope for a better future. This old bill still has an effect on minority families to this day. Again, tougher laws are not the answer; we need the lawmakers to call upon their humanity, showing empathy and promoting hope and opportunities for all, not just for minorities, but for disadvantaged and high-risk White people as well.

To Mrs. Clinton's credit, she has since apologized for using such words and expressed her regret; I applaud her for admitting she was wrong in her choice of words. Nowadays, if you said something in the past and you deeply regret it, you are still punished by the way of cancel culture. I believe when someone sees the error of their way, we should forgive them and let it go; remember, Jesus forgave us for our regretted past mistakes.

The next crime I would like to discuss is called White-collar crime; this is predominantly committed by educated White males. Now these are your superpredators, which are a sophisticated class of high-tech thieves.

These superpredators are the ones who cold-bloodedly calculate every move of their often vulnerable, elderly victims, not our young Black misguided youth, who in most cases don't understand the magnitude of what they are doing.

On the other hand, most White-collar predators do not come from a background of misfortune or a life of disparity; they are just downright greedy monsters.

I would describe White-collar crimes as lying, cheating, stealing, and taking advantage of the weak; in a nutshell, a thug. There is a full range of fraud committed by business and government professionals. These are not victimless crimes either; a single scam can destroy a company and devastate families by wiping out their life savings, eliminating pensions, and costing investors billions of dollars. How about Bernard Madoff's Ponzi scheme or the Lehman Brothers scandal? I call them high-tech thugs, evil-hearted men who destroy the life savings of families and rob senior citizens of their hard-earned money. This, in turn, denies them of the comfortable retirement they have earned, so they instead find themselves struggling from day to day to make ends meet, sometimes followed by chronic depression and suicidal tendencies. Meanwhile, these blood-sucking parasites drift away in a golden parachute to land on a retirement resort with pristine golf courses to live the country club lifestyle the remaining years of their life.

Crime in the 21st century has truly taken on a new meaning; it is time for the American people to take a stand together against crime, wherever you find it, and lock up those who wish to terrorize cities with their thuggish ways. As for those who desire to change and respect their fellow man, let us give them a hand up—not a handout—through education, rehabilitation, job training, and placement. Let us set them on the path of success, moving them into mainstream society with goals of becoming homeowners and taxpaying, law-abiding citizens who have transformed themselves from being a liability to an asset in their communities.

Why has crime increased so much over the last two generations? The number one reason is, just as I said earlier, due to a lack of knowledge of God. Even our government is encouraging people to abandon God as it tries to remove God from mainstream society and the educational system.

During my elementary school days, we would place our hands over our hearts and recite the Pledge of Allegiance as the first thing we did in class. This taught us early to be patriotic, support our country, believe that God stands guard over us, and assures our right to liberty and justice. Now our harmless Pledge of Allegiance is under attack by liberals who seem to think that it is unconstitutional to allow kids to mention God in school; when you take God out of the school system, crime will definitely increase because kids are not taught from the beginning the fear of God. Just three generations ago, God was allowed in schools. During that time, kids were shooting tiny paper spitballs through a straw in the classroom and the lunchroom for mischievous fun. But now they are shooting 9mms and semiautomatic weapons on school grounds and campuses. Just some fifty-plus years ago, there was a fear of God and respect for the teachers, who would correct you verbally or sometimes physically with a paddle. On top of that, the school would notify your parents, and when you got home, you received another paddling; by no means am I promoting corporal corrections, but rather teach students to respect rules. Back in the day, teachers were teaching us early in life that there are consequences for your actions and to respect the rule of law, such as the rule of do not steal. We cannot view stealing as no big deal; it is so big of a deal that it can rob you of your honor. And clearly, the lack of honor and respect is something we need to work on in our society. Most crimes start at home for kids; therefore, most crimes can be prevented at home with godly rearing and the message of love and respect for authority and for one another.

In Conclusion

Crime. Let's face it; there are certain segments of the population that are at high risk when it comes to crime, especially among residents of the inner city and the impoverished. Some are thugs, which is basically someone who is set on being a career criminal who commit acts of violence, who mugs, robs, hurts, and bullies innocent people for their own gain and may never change and should be locked up. Again, keep in mind a lot of high-risk youth simply need a hand up. Unfortunately, a vast amount of people across the world only see the crimes they commit and not the potentials they have. I believe they need to be brought out of life's desert of despair and transplanted into an oasis of hope and opportunity.

Must people across the world just need to be brought out of life's desert of despair and carried into an oasis of hope and opportunity. Without intervention, it is hard to escape this cycle of crime; it is not as simple as pulling yourself up by your bootstraps. These precious people really need our help. It is easy to sit back in our plush comfort zone and complain about the crime problem instead of helping to resolve it. Our government spends billions on proxy wars in the Middle East but won't spend a fraction of that on the war on poverty-related crimes in America; I'm sure you will agree it makes no sense. It seemed to me our government should help America first because this can potentially become a domestic security threat.

I may not have all the answers to these problems, but one thing I do know is that locking people up is not the answer. This only creates revolving juvenile detention and penitentiary doors. When a kid is in elementary school, and the teacher asks that popular question—what do you want to be when you grow up?—I do not know of any kid who would raise their hand in the air and reply, "I'm looking forward to becoming the world's best thug." I don't think so. Most of this behavior is spawned from their environments and combined with broken homes and absent fathers. I call them MIP: Missing in Parenthood. They are not true fathers; they are just sperm donors. It is sad to see these fathers missing during the years of parenthood—a time when a child's mind is a sponge, hungering for knowledge, love, and attention. Young boys need a father's guiding hand to usher them into adulthood.

As I said earlier, stopping crime begins at home, so I encourage you, as parents, to spend more time with your kids in bonding, loving on them, and teaching them to respect their fellow man. Teach them work ethics, humanitarian deeds, social skills, the need to earn their keep and pull their load in society. Teach them to never be a taker, rather always a giver. Above all things, teach them to fear God and to serve Him with all their heart, soul, and mind. In doing this, you will release into the world a good role model and a blessing to society.

CHAPTER FOUR
THE ECONOMY

    Please keep in mind this chapter is written in part from a visionary perspective.

    The economy seems to be America's primary focal point; the health of the economy is a major concern of every country. Depending on how the economy is faring determines for some people whether or not they spend their money. This is one of many factors that can lead to a recession, which is a period of general economic decline. A recession is typically accompanied by slow growth, such as a drop in the stock market, an increase in unemployment, and a decline in the housing market. If a recession continues long enough, it is often classified as a depression.

    Some believe there is no obvious cause of a recession, although overall blame generally falls on the federal leadership, often on either the president himself, the head of the Federal Reserve, or the entire legislature. Surely the government should not take full responsibility for a weak economy or recession. We should bear some of the blame for allowing the government and politicians to make such bad decisions with the taxpayers' money. These elected leaders control spending for the Federal Reserve and federal budget, which gives them some power to prevent and/or combat inflation. Our federal debt is so far out of control it is difficult to comprehend. To give you an idea of just how bad it is, the U.S. federal debt topped $28.43 trillion by the end of 2021; this is the largest in the world for a single country. It runs neck and neck with that of the European Union, which is an economic union of 27 countries. Now that is what I call incomprehensible. How did this occur? It is when the U.S. government has a deficit, and most of the deficit spending is covered by the government taking on new debt.

Let me tell you something, my friend: we are going about it the wrong way. We are borrowing money we cannot pay back. We are leaving our children in debt for generations to come, and that, my friend, is not fair. They try to fix it by raising taxes, which takes money from consumers and businesses, which are the lifeline of the economy. We are being overtaxed; the average working-class man pays 15% in taxes. Now let us say he gives 10% to his church or favorite charity on top of his tax obligation. That is 25% of his earnings gone already before he makes it to the bank. If he makes $100 per day, $25 is gone. Plus, there's gas money to get back and forth to work, say $15 per day for transportation cost. Total money gone before he spends a dime on his family is $40. So, true take-home pay is only $60 per day, which is something to think about. These are individuals who are economically stuck. I call them IESs, short for Individuals who are Economically Stuck. For the working-class person, I am talking about being stuck in a rut like Chuck and can't get up. Therefore, raising taxes is not the answer to pay for the government's out-of-control spending and its operation. Red Alert: the system is broken.

They use quick-fix tricks like the economic stimulus packages, supposedly designed to jump-start economic growth. A stimulus package is a sense of denial; it is just like having to jump-start your car every morning; one day, you go out to start it up, but it doesn't start due to the fact you never dealt with the underlying problems. Those who are mechanically inclined know that this approach will eventually lead to other problems.

You do not have to be the brightest star in the sky to realize that something is seriously wrong with our economic system. Our economy is built on a system in which we trade by the means of production that is controlled by private owners with the single goal of making immense, short-term profits. This is unlike socialism, which critiques capitalism by arguing that capitalism creates basic economic inequalities that limit human potential. Socialists maintain that capitalism is derived from a system of labor exploitation.

This concentrates wealth and power in the hands of a small segment of society that controls the means of production.

On the other hand, socialism is a system in which property and wealth distribution is subject to control by the community, state, or government. This leaves control of wealth up to a "Big Brother" to ensure that you receive your fair share. Therefore, you have no need for ownership in socialism. This system is defined as an economic theory, system, or movement in which the production and distribution of goods are done, owned, and shared by the citizens of a society.

Now, after understanding the process of socialism, who would want that kind of economic system? No thanks, right? But on the other hand, capitalism promotes a clear double standard, and some say Democrats lean toward programs that are prototypes of socialism. For example, let's look at the heated topic of affordable healthcare. Now, using the capitalist system, the healthcare insurance market makes healthcare inaccessible for most of the forty-five million reported uninsured Americans back in 2010, which has dropped since then, due to the Affordable Care Act, thanks in part to former President Barack Obama and his administration. Now, remember, capitalism describes an economic system that entails the ability of a private enterprise to produce products, goods, or services for a profit. Therefore, health insurance providers have the ability to set their own prices unless the government asserts regulatory pricing. If not, this makes hospitals, doctors, and pharmaceutical companies powerful lords over their free enterprise. This typically leads to inflated medical care costs that the average person cannot afford. This, in turn, puts the consumer into the infamous "Catch-22."

High Prices Equal High Cost of Living

Under capitalism, the product manufacturer gets to set their own price. In addition, prices are often driven by demand. Did you know that lobster was once used as prison food years ago? It is considered a scavenger. I call it the ocean cockroach. Years ago, people despised it, making it cheap and affordable to feed prisoners. But now, it is expensive and generally considered a delicacy. In the case of lobster, the market price has been set so high that the average family cannot afford a lobster dinner. The same is true with other goods and services that use cheap labor. Some companies use fair market labor to produce goods and then, in turn, sell them at astronomical prices.

In a capitalist economic system, I believe one should share wealth out of a sense of responsibility. In business dealings, we all should maintain basic ethical practices, especially toward those who help us get to where we are. Business owners should have some sense of moral responsibility to help the employees who help them to achieve success. And as far as those corporations who use illegal sweatshops to profit off their cheap labor—they should be ashamed of themselves before God. Some Americans see immigrants as a threat when they come to America. These precious people are tired of being used. Americans want to set up operations in their countries and make a profit off their backs but do not care for them to come to the U.S. and make some real money. You want your cake and eat it too. It does not work both ways; you want to eat all your cake and still have cake. In the present-day economy and job market, employee earnings typically do not match the cost of living. Current wages do not keep up with rising prices, thus putting them in a "Catch-22."

This phrase is from the novel *Catch-22* by Joseph Heller, which is about a World War II captain John Yossarian, a U.S. Army Air Force B-25 bombardier who became deranged from flying multiple bombing missions. He hoped, after meeting his quota, he would soon be relieved of duty. However, his superior officer kept adding more missions until he finally checked into the military hospital for mental evaluation on the grounds that people were conspiring to kill him.

Strictly speaking, a Catch-22 is "a problematic situation for which the only solution is denied by a circumstance inherent in the problem or by a rule." For example, losing something is typically a conventional problem; to solve it, one looks for the lost item until one finds it. On the other hand, if the thing lost is one's glasses, how can one find them without being able to see? If a person lacks work experience, no one will hire him, which means he cannot get a job to gain experience. If one does not have money, one can't invest to make money. The term "Catch-22" is also used more broadly to mean a tricky problem, a no-win, or absurd situation.

In *Catch-22*, Captain John Yossarian refuses to fly more missions out of fear for his life, citing a mental breakdown. But his superior officers refuse to believe that he is losing it. If someone is crazy, he can be discharged from the Army. But one has to apply for the discharge, and applying shows that one is *not* crazy; therefore, one cannot possibly be discharged for this reason. In a Catch-22, it is described this way:

> "There was only one catch and that was Catch-22, which specified that a concern for one's safety in the face of dangers that were real and immediate was the process of a rational mind. Orr [a bomber pilot and friend of Yossarian] was crazy and could be grounded. All he had to do was ask; and as soon as he did, he would no longer be crazy and would have to fly more missions. Orr would be crazy to fly more missions and sane if he didn't, but if he was sane, he had to fly them. If he flew them, he was crazy and didn't have to; but if he didn't want to, he was sane and had to. Yossarian was moved very deeply by the absolute simplicity of this clause of Catch-22 and let out a respectful whistle."

This ideology still sets a political and moral tone to this day. When you look at healthcare, it is clearly a Catch-22 for some. That occurs when you make too much to receive Medicaid benefits and make too little to afford private insurance. Let's say Brandon has a family of four, makes $3500 per month, and his private health insurance costs him $1800 per month without a government subsidy. Imagine he also pays $1500 per month for rent, leaving him with just $200 for all other bills and food. Here is a case in which he makes too much to qualify for government assistance and makes too little to afford health coverage on his own. In reality, he either needs government intervention, or the cost for health insurance needs to be lower.

If not, he is stuck in a Catch-22.

I label guys like Brandon as IESs—Individuals who are Economically Stuck. There are tons of IESs in the United States who need help.

This brings me back full circle to the economy. Our current economic system is hard on the average citizen. That is why sometimes we need our government to step in and help the American people. So, when looking at the heated debate over the Affordable Care Act (ACA), or so-called Obama Care, it's important to remember that it's not just Obama's Care; it's the *People's Care*. Just as Republicans and politicians have access to good healthcare, so should their constituents. For politicians to criticize the Obama Administration for trying to help those who find themselves in a Catch-22 situation is preposterous, especially when they never had a plan in place to help those in need, nor did they feel it was important enough to work toward one. Now they are saying we can do this, that, and the other. Guess what? It is too little, too late.

Again, I do not think that the ACA is the best way of going about making healthcare more accessible. I do not know any race of people that desires to receive government handouts. But I do know that, for millions of Americans, it is better than what they had previously, which was nothing. I believe that the American people want to be able to pay their own way, but sometimes it's not possible due to greed. So, what do we do for everybody to be able to afford the growing cost of living? Some ask, why not increase taxes on the rich to pay for certain programs? I ask, why should we penalize those who work hard and became successful and are living the American dream? Nonetheless, I do believe they should pay their fair share of taxes.

Some have suggested that the government should increase minimum wages, but will that really solve the problem? Well, let us test that theory. Right now, the minimum wage will gradually top $15 per hour. Remember, as we saw earlier in this chapter, that in a capitalist economic system, the owners of a company can raise prices on their goods and services at will, either to keep up with the growing cost or to be more lucrative.

In this case, prices will increase due to higher minimum wage. Let's use a scenario of tomato pickers: if the farmer must pay his pickers more money due to a minimum wage hike, in return, he must go up on the price of his tomatoes. So, what does that mean? It means the cost of your pizza will go up, and your spaghetti dinner will cost you more money at your favorite restaurant. The price for everything that is associated with tomatoes would go up. Hotel owners must pay housekeepers more money also, so now the room rates go up. The lumberyard owner must pay his workers more, so now lumber goes up, and this would cause the cost of home construction to go up.

Now imagine everything is all of a sudden inflated, and now the people who just got a minimum wage pay raise are back where they started. So, what do you do now? Go up on minimum wages again? You cannot index minimum wages faster than inflation. Now you are in a price-matching war for labor and production costs, which is known as tit-for-tat. This type of economic retaliation is ineffective. If we keep applying this old method, years from now, a fast-food worker will be making $25 per hour, making the cost for a large cheeseburger combo almost $20.

I have an economic system after which we can model our economy. Let us face it; the system in place now is broken. The only people getting ahead are the ones at the top. If we keep operating the way things are now, we will end up maintaining the status quo with the have and have-nots. Also, we need to keep in mind that with an increase in modern technology, jobs that exist today may be gone tomorrow.

To give you an idea of just how fast technology has advanced, look at the Wright Brothers' first flight in 1903. Sixty-six years later, Apollo 11 landed on the moon. From 1969 until 1997—twenty-eight years later—man landed on Mars through the Mars Rover Mission. All of this was achieved in the span of ninety-four years, and now we are in an era of private space travelers taking paid citizens to the edge of orbit. So, as you can see, technology is moving fast. It will eventually eliminate more and more jobs as we know them today. The need to reinvent our economy is a dire one.

To survive and compete in the 21st-century global market, we need dramatic reform now!

I present to you my new economic reform plan: the Nationwide Economy System of Traders (NEST). Its goal is to achieve worldwide economic domination. It is a simple formula. For it to work, the American people must be on board with it, along with the lawmakers, to sign it into law. The economist must push for a new law that would convert our current economy to the new systematic economy standards, called the Nationwide Economy System of Traders (NEST), which could mean financial freedom for many Americans.

Here is how it works. The first thing we must do is bring the cost of living down to the point where the U.S. is in the top three countries with the lowest cost of living in the world. Lower prices mean lower labor rates, which result in low costs of production and lower prices for goods and services.

From there, we would use big incentive programs to lure back the corporations that turned their back on America, who outsourced jobs to other countries; former President Trump was on the right track by promoting corporations to return to America by offering lower corporate taxes. I believe, in some cases with U.S. corporations, their actions were a simple choice of survival rather than an outright betrayal. At this point, it really does not matter; what matters is that we get multinational corporations to come back to the U.S. We do that by reversing what caused them to leave in the first place: their struggle to ensure a healthy financial bottom line. Let's face it; people go into business to make money, not to lose money. So, for starters, the government should offer a competitive, worldwide business tax rate—less than any other foreign country—and offer land for $1 for a hundred years for new factory construction or whatever it takes to lure them back.

Factually speaking, the government is losing lots of money, according to the Congressional Research Service. Corporate tax revenue in 2013 was down to less than a third of what it was at its post-World War II peak in 1952.

Corporate tax was the reason for so many companies moving overseas, along with cheaper labor that resulted in huge profits, as the U.S. tax rate used to be one of the highest among developed economies.

Many big U.S. companies are swimming in untaxed cash, but with a catch. Since U.S. multinational companies only owe U.S. tax on foreign earnings when they bring the money back to the U.S., of course, that wouldn't make much business sense, so, instead, they hide billions of dollars in offshore cash stashes.

So, we could offer a 7% corporate tax rate that increases 2% every ten years, which would eventually max out at 3% less than the going foreign rate. Whether you know it or not, the average global corporate tax rate is around 24–30 percent. That would make America the most attractive place and best place to do business, with a combination of lower corporate taxes and low hourly wages, which could be offset by low cost of living.

After using unbeatable incentives to bring back American corporations, we need to seriously rebuild our outdated infrastructure in order to function in the 21st-century economy; the first thing is to invest in renewable energy to limit our dependency on foreign oil. We need to invest in technology and in an aggressive, nationwide education system where all American citizens can receive a top-notch education at an affordable cost. This represents a huge investment in the future of our economy; this way, we will be able to develop the world's brightest scientists, engineers, computer software developers, etc.

Next, we should rebuild our roads, bridges, tunnels, and transportation systems that connect us from coast to coast. This should consist of two transportation systems connecting the East Coast with the West Coast to move people and goods in half the time and at half the price of their current transit rates. First, we need a high-speed rail that is second to none around the world, like the Japanese Maglev Train. This is a transport method that uses magnetic levitation to move vehicles without touching the ground. The Maglev vehicle travels along a guideway using magnets to create both lift and propulsion, thereby reducing friction and allowing higher speeds. It is known as the bullet train, with speeds of up to 268 MPH. Let's say you want to travel from the East Coast to the West Coast by car, roughly a 2700-mile trip at

65 miles an hour. It takes 41 hours to get to the West Coast; this would take approximately 4–5 days to drive by car driving 8–10 hours per day. By traveling 268 MPH on high-speed magnetic rails, a person could make the trip in about 10 hours.

A second system will follow alongside it for passenger cars and tractor-trailers, similar to the German Autobahn, with unlimited speeds and four arteries that connect at one-fourth, one-half, and three-fourths to allow the other parts of the United States to enter and exit for a toll fee to travel on this nationwide U.S. expressway.

Next, we would work on the NEST program by promoting it as a new and innovative concept. By joining this program, employers and employees will benefit from a new and unbelievably low-cost economy in which prices would be far lower than in the past. Our prices would bottom out at the following examples:

- Bread, $0.15,
- Dozen eggs, $0.20,
- Potatoes, $0.40/10 lb. bag,
- Porter House Steak, $1.00/lb,
- Chicken, $0.50/lb,
- Apples, $0.40/2 lb. bag,
- Sugar, $0.50/5 lb. bag,
- Average rent for three bedrooms, $200.00 a month,
- Average mortgage for four bedrooms, $150.00 a month.

These were prices of goods in the fifties. It is possible to turn back the economic clock, but everyone must agree to work for less and sell for less to enjoy the benefits of such low prices. Therefore, we can live for a lot less.

This will create one of the lowest costs of living in the world; this will encourage American corporations to return to America.

This would likely be followed by foreign companies that can't compete. Ultimately, they will have us making more products for them instead of them making products for us, which in turn would increase American exports exponentially. This would lead to American-made products that are safer, better, and cheaper than those made in other countries.

With this system in place, we would have a booming economy like never seen before. Let's face it; if we don't overhaul our economy, it's doomed to fail. Do not be fooled by the up-and-down unemployment rate; plus, due to the pandemic, the unemployment rate has been put in an unprecedented position. According to God's plan, when a deadly plague, virus, or pandemic breaks out, God's Word teaches that we should quarantine, which calls for worldwide cooperation and sacrifices from each country. This would help stabilize the country much faster and cheaper than vaccines alone. Had we quarantined corporately and toughed it out, we would not be battling the ongoing infectious rate to this day. Maybe we should take a lesson from the Chinese on how to eradicate viruses cheaper and efficiently, so we can put the economy back on track. They have ordered another mandatory lockdown to try to obtain a zero-infection report; it won't be long before their economy is booming again while we are still struggling with the pandemic. I am sorry to say this because I know that's not what people want to hear; however, more people will die because Americans are spoiled and have no patience. Also, we are primarily depending upon vaccinations and not common sense. Again, cut the head of the snake off, and the body will die; we have only been cutting the tail off, which means the tail will grow back as the viruses keep coming back. A virus cannot replicate alone; viruses must infect cells and use components of the host cell to make copies of themselves. So, quarantine is the cheapest and fastest way to stop a virus in its tracks, along with a unilateral effort upon initial outbreak discovery, to isolate the virus; not a government cover-up, so we can continue business as usual and ignorantly spread the virus. Of course, along with common sense practices, such as medical treatment, preventive measures, patience, and border closure. Now, back to the economy. The economy will never be stable unless significant changes are made; we have two choices. We can continue along our current course by raising the cost of living and minimum wages until it hits an all-time high, or we can become one of the lowest cost-of-living countries in the world to gain world economic dominance.

In Conclusion

Economy. How does God feel about His children's economy? Here's what God's Word says about how to have a blessed economy:

> *And it shall come to pass, if thou shalt hearken diligently unto the voice of the LORD thy God, to observe and to do all his commandments which I command thee this day, that the LORD thy God will set thee on high above all nations of the earth: And all these blessings shall come on thee, and overtake thee, if thou shalt hearken unto the voice of the LORD thy God. Blessed shalt thou be in the city, and blessed shalt thou be in the field. Blessed shall be the fruit of thy body, and the fruit of thy ground, and the fruit of thy cattle, the increase of thy kine, and the flocks of thy sheep. Blessed shall be thy basket and thy store. Blessed shalt thou be when thou comest in, and blessed shalt thou be when thou goest out. The LORD*

shall cause thine enemies that rise up against thee to be smitten before thy face: they shall come out against thee one way, and flee before thee seven ways. The LORD shall command the blessing upon thee in thy storehouses, and in all that thou settest thine hand unto; and he shall bless thee in the land which the LORD thy God giveth thee. The LORD shall establish thee an holy people unto himself, as he hath sworn unto thee, if thou shalt keep the commandments of the LORD thy God, and walk in his ways. And all people of the earth shall see that thou art called by the name of the LORD; and they shall be afraid of thee. And the LORD shall make thee plenteous in goods, in the fruit of thy body, and in the fruit of thy cattle, and in the fruit of thy ground, in the land which the LORD sware unto thy fathers to give thee. The LORD shall open unto thee his good treasure, the heaven to give the rain unto thy land in his season, and to bless all the work of thine hand: and thou shalt lend unto many nations, and thou shalt not borrow. And the LORD shall make thee the head, and not the tail; and thou shalt be above only, and thou shalt not be beneath; if that thou hearken unto the commandments of the LORD thy God, which I command thee this day, to observe and to do them: And thou shalt not go aside from any of the words which I command thee this day, to the right hand, or to the left, to go after other gods to serve them. But it shall come to pass, if thou wilt not hearken unto the voice of the LORD thy God, to observe to do all his commandments and his statutes which I command thee this day; that all these curses shall come upon thee, and overtake thee:Cursed shalt thou be in the city, and cursed shalt thou be in the field. Cursed shall be thy basket and thy store. Cursed shall be the fruit of thy

> *body, and the fruit of thy land, the increase of thy kine, and the flocks of thy sheep. Cursed shalt thou be when thou comest in, and cursed shalt thou be when thou goest out. The LORD shall send upon thee cursing, vexation, and rebuke, in all that thou settest thine hand unto for to do, until thou be destroyed, and until thou perish quickly; because of the wickedness of thy doings, whereby thou hast forsaken me. The LORD shall make the pestilence cleave unto thee, until he have consumed thee from off the land, whither thou goest to possess it. The LORD shall smite thee with a consumption, and with a fever, and with an inflammation, and with an extreme burning, and with the sword, and with blasting, and with mildew; and they shall pursue thee until thou perish. And thy heaven that is over thy head shall be brass, and the earth that is under thee shall be iron. The LORD shall make the rain of thy land powder and dust: from heaven shall it come down upon thee, until thou be destroyed. The LORD shall cause thee to be smitten before thine enemies: thou shalt go out one way against them, and flee seven ways before them: and shalt be removed into all the kingdoms of the earth. And thy carcase shall be meat unto all fowls of the air, and unto the beasts of the earth, and no man shall fray them away.*
>
> Deuteronomy 28:1–26

Here we find God, telling His people, if you obey Him and keep His commandments, you and your economy will flourish with blessings, and the nation will prosper. On the other hand, if you do not obey and serve Him, your economy will be cursed for your disobedience and sins.

We all have heard of the old saying that the definition of insanity is doing the same thing over and over and expecting different results. Continuing to operate using our current, outdated economic system will lead to self-destruction in the not-so-distant future. Our economy is so fragile that any major interference can hurt it, such as a stock market crash, sudden high-interest rates, or another devastating pandemic like the COVID-19 virus or a catastrophic terrorist attack. This brings us to the issue of our weak open border security. There is no doubt we need to increase security along our borders because the world is not going to get any better. There is a debate over should we have a border wall? I would ask the Democrat Party, why not for now? Don't you have some type of security around your home? I believe we need a border wall today, but not necessarily tomorrow; especially with technology and innovation on the rise, walls will one day be obsolete. However, adding more security will not assure us 100% protection because terrorists are like mosquitoes at a backyard barbecue party; you can have all the mosquito repellents in the world and a giant electric bug zapper, but still, someone will eventually get bitten. Once you kill the one that bit you, there are many more lurking around in the distant backyard woods, waiting for you to let your guard down. The only 100% guarantee of our protection, welfare, and prosperity as a nation is God. According to Proverbs 16:7, God is the one who can protect us against terrorism. It states:

When a man's ways please the LORD, he maketh even his enemies to be at peace with him.

The point is, America needs to get back to pleasing God; then, He will cause our enemies to be at peace with us.

Therefore, I say we should put God first and step out on faith to rebuild in the name of The Lord our God. Because Psalm 127:1 says:

> *Except the LORD build the house, they labour in vain that build it: except the LORD keep the city, the watchman waketh but in vain.*

God bless America.

CHAPTER FIVE
RACISM IN AMERICA

It is the diversity of America that makes her so beautiful. However, attached to diversity sometimes comes racism and discrimination. To understand racism in America, you must, indeed, start from the beginning. According to history, in 1492, there was a well-financed trip sponsored by Queen Isabella of Spain for Christopher Columbus to find rich new territories and a new sailing route to India and China, then known as the Indies. On the contrary to one's belief, there is another ambiguous version of this story found in American history. Some historians believe that Jews financed his trip for the sole purpose of finding them a new homeland after the expulsion of the Jews from Spain by Queen Isabella and King Ferdinand in 1492. This was a move aimed to expel over 800,000 Jews who refused to convert to Catholicism. Long after he set sail, Columbus inadvertently discovered a new continent that was later named after another explorer, Amerigo Vespucci, known today as America. Eventually, settlers came in search of a new and better way of life, away from war-torn countries, poverty, dictatorships, and religious persecution.

They arrived after hearing stories of untold riches and land; this prompted immigration from many other countries from all parts of Europe, such as the Spaniards, British, Portuguese, Frenchmen, Dutch, and Scottish. Many of them established empires and colonies spanning from Canada to South America. They, unfortunately, brought with them not only seeds, spices, melons, livestock, and technology but also diseases, which wiped out a large percentage of the indigenous populations. Settlers viciously conquered native tribes through relentless conquest for land, precious metals, and minerals, such as gold and silver. This, of course, led to the darker side of America's history.

It is one thing to come to the New World to seek a better way of life and religious liberties, but it's another thing for the European Caucasians to rape, slaughter, and enslave so-called savage people merely to exploit them (indeed, it makes you wonder who were the savages). Fortunately, Queen Isabella ordered the freedom of all the Mexican Native Indian slaves held by their Spaniard captors upon converting to Catholicism. However, I would like to expose some hidden or forgotten American history. Native American slave trafficking spanned from Canada to South America and ended in the early 1900s, especially during the Good Year Tire rubber boom era. The Amazon people were enslaved, raped, beaten, and forced to work in the rainforest, cutting down rubber trees. Good Year used a process called vulcanization that makes the latex harder to form a rubber substance for automobile tires. As one can see, many people have suffered horribly for hundreds of years by a system of oppression and greed. This is to say, "Get all I can, while I can, no matter how I can and can all I get."

Back in the early 1600s, after a decline in free labor carried out by natives, the idea was born to import African slaves to meet the demand for labor. They were kidnapped and sometimes sold by African tribal warlords themselves to White slave traders. From there, they were made into cargo transported across the Atlantic, known as the Transatlantic Slave Trade. The Africans were mercilessly shackled to one another in cramped quarters. Many died during the mid-Atlantic passage due to several conditions, mainly disease and starvation. Many slaves grew too depressed to eat or function due to their loss of freedom, family, security, and their own humanity. Some, after arriving here and being auctioned off, felt it might have been better if they had died than to be abused at the hands of a cruel slave master. This abuse included derogatory names, like the N-word, severe beatings, and rape. That same slaveholder would sneak down to the slave quarters after dinner, perhaps telling his wife he was going out to have a cigar and get some fresh air, and instead raped the young slave women, which was common for slave owners. You can clearly see the hypocrisy of those White men; although our ancestors were not good enough to eat with them and be their equals, they were certainly good enough to sleep with them.

Often slave women became pregnant from these rapes by their masters, who then placed their own flesh and blood out in the field as slaves. That was largely how we, as African Americans, became a race of mixed shades because of White genes. Therefore, we are brothers, just of another mother.

There are not too many purebred people in America. Most of us are mixed with genes from other races. Some of our ancestors are homogenous, such as the Nubians, from which some African American slaves were direct descendants. Nubia is in southern Egypt, where Black people ruled for thousands of years as kings and queens over advanced civilizations with math, science, medicine, and the arts. Even today, museums display paintings and artwork of great ancient Black cultures.

There are large monuments of Black pharaohs along the Nile River to this day that have been disfigured. Now, as America grew with more prospectors, the demand for more land and territorial rights grew also, which brings us to another dark chapter in American history called "The Trail of Tears." This was the forced relocation of Native American Nations following the Indian Removal Act of 1830. This removal included members of the Cherokee, Muskogee, Seminole, Chickasaw, and the Choctaw Nations, who chose not to assimilate into their occupier's society and culture. Around 6,000 native people died from exposure, disease, and starvation, only to make way for many White settlers who encroached on native lands. That's a nice way of saying they stole the land.

As you can see, many people have suffered horribly at the hand of the European colonist in the course of forming this new nation. The stakes got higher once development and agriculture grew profitable on commodities such as tobacco and sugar. Great Britain wanted more of the bounty and therefore imposed taxes on colonies, which spawned the Revolutionary War. Thanks be to God, the Americans won. The Revolutionary War was followed by another dark side of American history, known as the Civil War.

There were thirty-four states at that time, of which seven southern slave states individually declared their secession from the United States and formed their own Confederate States of America. They were identified as the Confederacy, or the South, versus the Union, or the North. After four years of fighting, the Union emerged from the war-torn, smoky battlefields as the victor at a high cost; brothers slaughtered brothers because of different ideologies on how the new country should be established. I hope and trust we have learned a lesson from this era, as our democracies have been tested repeatedly, even recently, in the wake of January 6.

After the Civil War, what came next was the Reconstruction Era, the processes of restoring national unity as the Founding Fathers had envisioned it as one nation. Even though the Pledge of Allegiance was written long after the Reconstruction and the

Constitution, we have come to understand more clearly the Pledge of Allegiance, which I must say is powerful:

"I pledge allegiance to the Flag of the United States of America, and to the Republic for which it stands, one Nation under God, indivisible, with liberty and justice for all."

In 1954, in response to the Communist threat of the times, President Eisenhower encouraged Congress to add the words "under God," creating the thirty-one-word pledge we say today. We, as Americans, should stick together, as one nation under God, and never be divided along racial lines. The Bible declares:

> *And if a kingdom be divided against itself, that kingdom cannot stand. And if a house be divided against itself, that house cannot stand.*
>
> Mark 3:24–25

The South wanted to divide the nation, while the North wanted one nation. I believe that it should be just as the pledge of allegiance stated: "One nation under God." But unfortunately, we are increasingly seeing division along racial lines and in our current political climate, with Republicans and Democrats revealing a deeply divided house. I am convinced that some of the Founding Fathers of our great nation had giant hearts and a passion for the success of the nation and the prosperity of the people. They profoundly stated in the Declaration of Independence:

> "We hold these truths to be self-evident, that all men are created equal, that they are endowed by their Creator with certain unalienable Rights, that among these are Life, Liberty and the pursuit of Happiness."

The idea of this declaration was put to the test when it was challenged concerning slavery. If America was to live up to its decree, slavery had to be abolished. And after many years of struggling and debating, believe it or not—for those in the African American community—part of the credit should go to former President Abraham Lincoln and the Republican Party for ending slavery. Mr. Lincoln became the United States' 16th President in 1861, issuing the Emancipation Proclamation, which declared forever free those slaves within the Confederacy in 1863.

I believe there is not enough credit and recognition given to all the good-hearted White people who stood on the right side of history and helped put an end to the evils of slavery.

Unfortunately, when most minorities think of European colonization, what comes to mind are the heartless, cruel oppressors, but somehow, history has overlooked the genuine, God-fearing settlers with good intentions who coexisted with the natives of the land and opposed slavery. This is true, just as the modern-day White party opposed slavery during the 1850s and formed a coalition party called the G.O.P.—the Grand Old Party, which came into existence in 1854 to fight the Kansas-Nebraska Act. This Act tried to extend slavery into its territorial states to promote aggressive modernization and economic growth. Praise God Almighty!—that slavery was abolished in 1865 after the Civil War. During the Civil War, it has been said former slaves were granted 40+/- acres and a mule by Union General William T. Sherman, who believed former slaves had a constitutional right to own the property confiscated from their former masters. This act, known as The Freeman's Bureau Act, allowed some of the land to be given back to former slave owners who leased it to sharecroppers after it was repealed. Most Blacks acquired land through private transactions. Unfortunately, Blacks never received any form of reparation, unlike many other races, who experienced racial injustice, who received some form of reparation. African Americans never received any form of reparation from our government for its wrongful acts of slavery against humanity. Even to this day, African Americans are overlooked when it comes down to granting some form of reparation. Many Black people support the Democratic Party, who have no idea how anti-God this party really is; also, you would think since the Black community religiously supports the Democrat Party, they would offer the Black community reparation or financial grievance for the mistreatments of our ancestors, but instead, the same man you voted for, President Joe Biden, and his administration have suggested to offer over $400,000 in reparation to undocumented immigrants who crossed the borders illegally for their mistreatment. This should be viewed as a slap in the face for the Black communities and pastors who voted for him. You would think he would have said also it's time to make a wrong, right? That's long overdue for the injustice that was inflicted upon Black people through the Transatlantic Slave Trade. It seems like this would be the right time to make some type of offer of reparation for Black people, too. Republican President Ronald Reagan signed into law the Civil Liberties Act of 1988, which officially apologized for the internment on behalf of the U.S. government and authorized a payment of $20,000 (equivalent to $44,000 in 2020) to each former Japanese internee who was still alive when the act was passed. Also, Native Americans receive government grants for the injustice and mistreatment that was inflicted upon them. To this day, Black people still support the Democrat Party, and all they have given you is empty promises. More importantly, what we need now is more economic opportunity and racial equality.

Now, back to the Kansas-Nebraska Act, which was fiercely opposed by the G.O.P. Because the use of free slave labor would cause a cost-effect for small businesses with paid laborers, most of the Republican Party was made up of factory workers, farmers, businessmen, small business owners, professionals, Protestants, northern Whites, and African Americans. Over the years, African Americans have gravitated away from the Republican Party, known as the G.O.P., especially during the Great Depression and the Roosevelt presidency. Franklin Roosevelt was famously known for his New Deal Act, which lasted from 1932 to 1964 and was based on many social programs, some good and some bad. Some of these programs were needed, while there were others that needed to be done away with, even to this day, doing more harm than good, such as widespread welfare that was meant to be a temporary relief for those affected by the depression. And now, this has become a long-standing social and economic crutch for both Whites and Blacks. There's a large misconception when it comes to Blacks on welfare; in fact, Whites are the biggest beneficiaries when it comes to government safety-net programs like Temporary Assistance for Needy Families, commonly referred to as welfare. That, unfortunately, in many cases, leads to generations of poverty-stricken people. I call it the generational curse of welfare. We need to reform our entitlement programs and move from welfare to workfare through economic growth. And, of course, empowering the recipients with education and job training to build them a viable future without the need for government subsidy.

Now, after a brief history of how America, the melting pot, came to be, unfortunately, African Americans arrived not as free men but as slaves. Just for the record, the African American community holds no grudges against White people concerning the slave trade because it was not you who committed these heinous acts against our ancestors.

We don't quite understand why God allowed it, but one thing is for sure: God doesn't make mistakes. God has a way of turning something bad into something good. However, the problem we wrestle with now is the ongoing injustice system we face every day.

America cries that there's no money to build schools in the inner cities, although this nation finds money to build more prisons to incarcerate a disproportionate number of minorities and spends billions of dollars to fight proxy wars in the Middle East. At the same time, we can't fund the war on poverty and economic and social disparity in the U.S., which indicates that something is wrong with this picture.

As a descendant of Africa, I'm proud to be an American, despite the dark history against my people. We were held back for a long time, but as of today, no one is holding us back from succeeding. This is true, even though there is still discrimination and a general lack of opportunities. The only person who can hold a Black man back is himself. We can't blame White people for our problems, for those who seem to think so. Now that we have that clear, let's look at some of the real underlying problems that cause racism.

Racial division is still being taught by the old-school regime, the Jim Crow, White separatist groups, and the KKK, who continue to teach separatism, which promotes division in America. Eventually, they will all die off, and hopefully, their children won't continue to pass on such poisonous doctrine to future generations. There's a study called CRT Critical Race Theory; this is their statement concerning their organization's purpose:

> "Critical race theory (CRT) is a body of legal scholarship and an academic movement of US civil-rights scholars and activists who seek to examine the intersection of race and US law and to challenge mainstream American liberal approaches to racial justice. CRT examines social, cultural, and legal issues primarily as they relate to race and racism in the US."

However, I do not support this work and believe it should be banned from all schools' curriculums because of the complexity of it, causing a big misunderstanding among many people, especially the students. Let kids be kids; they know what to do when they see something that's not right, and the majority of them will stand up and speak out against bullying and racial rhetoric. Furthermore, most schools already have tools to educate kids concerning racism, such as Black History Month, so, hands off the kids. Adults and organizations like critical race theory (CRT) need to stop fueling the fire in the hearts and minds of children concerning racial division. Again, let kids be kids; they don't need all the extra stress while trying to obtain a good education. Today's kids are very smart and residual; they will figure out how to build a more inclusive, safer generation to come.

Neither do I support Black Lives Matter (BLM); the Black Lives Matter movement is far from what people have been led to believe. It started out as a protest for justice for minorities in wake of George Zimmerman's acquittal in the death of Trayvon Martin. However, it has evolved into a lucrative and personal agenda for the liberal Lesbian founders and members. Some of their protests involve looting and arson on innocent, hardworking business owners; whatever happened to peaceful protesting? Personally, I haven't seen anything that the Black Lives Matter movement has done to better the lives of the Black community; it seems to me this organization has caused more division among fellow Americans than anything. They are calling for defunding the police; this is nothing but reckless rhetoric. To defund the police puts their lives at a higher risk due to lack of resources; police lives matter, too. On the contrary, we need the police in the Black community more than anyone else, especially with the inner-city's high crime rates. Also, business owners need protection from the lawless smash and grab groups that are breaking into department stores and strong-arm taking merchandise at will. Where are the founders of Black Lives Matter when we see Black people committing organized crimes on national TV? Why aren't they out protesting them? If anyone needs to be defunded, it should be the Black Lives Matter organization; they have not done a thing significant and impactful to help the Black community. I am happy to say that our organization, Love Your Neighbor America (LYNA.ORG), has a solution to help combat crime in America that would help all people in the job market, especially those that are at high risk. This concept will help end the labor shortage in America, putting people back to work and thus, increasing economic growth through production of goods and services. It will also promote a better and safer policing in Black communities. I would be more than happy to sit down and share this plan with anyone who's willing to listen.

They use the phrase "Black Lives Matter," someone else said "All Lives Matter," and another said, "All Lives Can't Matter Until Black Lives Matter." This phrase was coined due to the long history of inequality and injustice that Black communities have received, especially when an unarmed Black man is unjustifiably killed by a White police officer who walks away free. The statistics do not lie; this is a serious problem.

So, because Black Lives Do Matter, I challenge the Black community to help put an end to Black-on-Black Crime where we are killing each other at an alarming rate. If we, The Black Communities, value our lives as we say, then we should focus on Black-on-Black Crime just as much as we focus on the injustice of a White police officer gunning down an unarmed Black man. I challenge the Black Lives Matter founders to go down in the gang-infested Black neighborhoods and protests and call for a truce to put an end to Black-on-Black crime. There are too many communities that are committing such atrocities against each other. Undeniably this gives the Black community a bad reputation among Americans and other countries; we are bigger and better than this. We can put an end to Black-on-Black Crime with the right help and attitude, and respect for each other along with love and unity. So, instead of destroying each other, why not work together to build up each other? This can begin by pulling your brothers and sisters out of the wilderness of despair and setting them on the road of hope and opportunity.

One of the most secretive questions in American homes today is: what color were they? We ask this question because, deep down inside, we feel that it's important to know when it comes to who's right or wrong regarding a matter of an incident. If our teenage son gets pulled over by a cop while driving, we want to know the color of the cop. Unfortunately, color sometimes plays a role in our day-to-day decisions. To show you a clearer picture of how color influences some of us in our decision-making, I would like to use two high-profile court cases. Let's start with the trial of O. J. Simpson, who was accused of murdering his wife, Nicole, and her friend, Ron Goldman. I have no doubt in my mind that O. J. Simpson murdered his wife and Ron Goldman, but unfortunately, he was found not guilty by a jury of his peers, in which the majority happened to be Black. Out of twelve jurors, nine were Black, one was Hispanic, and two were White.

The racial composition of the jury was strongly influenced by the decision of the prosecution to file the case in downtown Los Angeles rather than, as usual, in the jurisdiction where the crime occurred. This was a tremendous mistake on the prosecutor's part. Now, had the case been filed in Santa Monica, the jury would have been mostly White. This would mean that O. J. would have certainly been found guilty of double homicide, with life in prison or possibly the death penalty. But because the jury was a Black majority, he got away with murder, even though there were mounds of evidence against him.

When the jury read the verdict, "not guilty," O. J. and his lawyers were shocked and judging from the look on their faces, they themselves couldn't believe they had won the case. It's sad to say, but I remember hearing someone say, "I don't care whether he's guilty or not, just as long as White people got a taste of the racism and injustice we have experienced for four hundred years." I replied that two wrongs don't make a right, furthermore, that's not the right attitude one should have. We shouldn't seek twisted revenge on the innocent but embrace the idea of equal justice under the law for all people regardless of race or gender.

Now let's compare the George Zimmerman and Trayvon Martin case with the O. J. Simpson case. We will begin with the initial facts: the transcript of Mr. Zimmerman's 911 call to the Sanford Police Department.

> *Dispatcher: Sanford Police Department...*
> *Zimmerman: Hey, we've had some break-ins in my neighborhood, and there's a real suspicious guy, uh, [near] Retreat View Circle, um, the best address I can give you is 111 Retreat View Circle. This guy looks like he's up to no good, or he's on drugs or something. It's raining and he's just walking around, looking about.*
> *Dispatcher: Ok, and this guy, is he white, black, or Hispanic?*
> *Zimmerman: He looks black.*
> *Dispatcher: Did you see what he was wearing?*
> *Zimmerman: Yeah. A dark hoodie, like a grey hoodie, and either jeans or sweatpants and white tennis shoes. He's [unintelligible], he was just staring...*
> *Dispatcher: Ok, he's just walking around the area...*
> *Zimmerman:... looking at all the houses.*
> *Dispatcher: Ok...*
> *Zimmerman: Now he's just staring at me.*
> *Dispatcher: Ok—you said it's 1111 Retreat View? Or 111?*
> *Zimmerman: That's the clubhouse...*
> *Dispatcher: That's the clubhouse, do you know what the—he's near the clubhouse right now?*
> *Zimmerman: Yeah, now he's coming towards me.*
> *Dispatcher: Ok.*
> *Zimmerman: He's got his hand in his waistband. And he's a Black male.*
> *Dispatcher: How old would you say he looks?*
> *Zimmerman: He's got button on his shirt, late teens.*
> *Dispatcher: Late teens, ok.*

Zimmerman: Something's wrong with him. Yup, he's coming to check me out, he's got something in his hands, I don't know what his deal is.
Dispatcher: Just let me know if he does anything, ok.
Zimmerman: How long until you get an officer over here?
Dispatcher: Yeah, we've got someone on the way. Just let me know if this guy does anything else.
Zimmerman: Ok. These... they always get away. When you come to the clubhouse you come straight in and make a left. Actually, you would go past the clubhouse.
Dispatcher: So, it's on the left-hand side from the clubhouse?
Zimmerman: No, you go in straight through the entrance and then you make a left... uh, you go straight in, don't turn, and make a left...he's running.
Dispatcher: He's running? Which way is he running?
Zimmerman: Down towards the other entrance to the neighborhood.
Dispatcher: Which entrance is that that he's heading towards?
Zimmerman: The back entrance... [unintelligible]...
Dispatcher: Are you following him?
Zimmerman: Yeah.
Dispatcher: Ok, we don't need you to do that.
Zimmerman: Ok.
Dispatcher: Alright, sir, what is your name?
Zimmerman: George... He ran.
Dispatcher: Alright, George, what's your last name?
Zimmerman: Zimmerman.
Dispatcher: And, George, what's the phone number you're calling from?
Zimmerman: [redacted]
Dispatcher: Alright, George, we do have them on the way, do you want to meet with the officer when they get out there?
    Zimmerman: Alright, where you going to meet with them at?
Zimmerman: If they come in through the gate, tell them to go straight past the clubhouse, and uh, straight past the clubhouse and make a left, and then they go past the mailboxes, that's my truck... [unintelligible]

> ...
> Dispatcher: What address are you parked in front of?
> Zimmerman: I don't know. It's a cut through so I don't know the address.
> Dispatcher: Okay, do you live in the area?
> Zimmerman: Yeah, I... [unintelligible]...
> Dispatcher: What's your apartment number?
> Zimmerman: It's a home it's 1950, oh crap, I don't want to give it all out. I don't know where this kid is.
> Dispatcher: Okay, do you want to just meet with them right near the mailboxes then?
> Zimmerman: Yeah, that's fine.
> Dispatcher: Alright, George, I'll let them know to meet you around there, okay?
> Zimmerman: Actually, could you have them call me and I'll tell them where I'm at?
> Dispatcher: Okay, yeah, that's no problem.
> Zimmerman: Should I give you my number or you got it?
> Dispatcher: Yeah, I got it
> Zimmerman: Yeah, you got it.
> Dispatcher: Ok, no problem, I'll let them know to call you when you're in the area.
> Zimmerman: Thanks.
> Dispatcher: You're welcome.

In a nutshell of what took place that fatal, rainy night on February 26, 2012, a wannabe cop, George Zimmerman, cowardly ended the life of an innocent kid in cold blood. When you read the transcript, you can clearly recognize that Zimmerman had already cast judgment on Trayvon as a perpetrator. From the transcript, it appears that Zimmerman's adrenaline was running high at this point. He assumed Trayvon was an unwelcome intruder and killed him for no reason, but in fact, Martin was coming from a 7/11, where he had bought some Skittles and an Arizona Iced Tea; that's what he had in his hand, not a weapon. I've heard of unfair fights, such as someone having a knife at a gunfight, but Skittles and a can of tea? I mean, really. Last I heard, it's not a crime to be Black and walk through Zimmerman's neighborhood with a hoodie on for protection from the rain. He was on his way to his father's fiancée's house, which was in the same neighborhood. It was Zimmerman who began stalking Martin because, as he stated in the 911 call, "he looks like he's up to no good." Not only was Trayvon Martin racially profiled, but he was stalked and prejudged. I'm sure at this point, the kid was fearful for his life, so he called his girlfriend and informed her that a stranger was following him. Trayvon didn't know that Zimmerman was the community watchman. In fact, he had no idea who Zimmerman was. Therefore, Trayvon took off running, and Zimmerman pursued him against the order of the Sanford Police dispatcher, who advised him to stand down and wait for the police, which is the proper protocol.

Zimmerman ignored these orders and continued to pursue him. That's when Trayvon decided to stand his ground. Unfortunately, during the altercation, cowardly George Zimmerman, who provoked the entire incident, shot Trayvon in cold blood. Once Trayvon knew he was shot, Zimmerman testified that Trayvon yelled out, "You shot me," meaning he was completely shocked and taken by surprise. Zimmerman, who was almost twice Martin's size, was getting his behind kicked by a little kid, and he started wimping out and couldn't take it. So, he pulled out his gun and shot innocent, unarmed Trayvon Martin. All Zimmerman had to do was tap out and identify himself, and it would have been the end of the confrontation. But instead, he senselessly shot Trayvon.

There have been countless numbers of people who have been beaten worse than that at a bar fight, but they didn't kill anybody. All Zimmerman received was a few scratches and bruises. Normally, a person would realize they got their behind whipped and go on about their way.

Now to bring this to full circle, the case goes to trial with a predominantly white jury—almost the exact reverse of the O. J. Simpson jury—with eleven whites, one mixed Black/Hispanic. The jury allowed him to get away with murder. And shortly after the trial, Zimmerman had several run-ins with the law. Numerous women who he was involved with have since spoken out about his abusive behavior. He even threatened his ex-wife with a handgun. Now that his true colors have come out, it's too late. Unfortunately, the jury couldn't see through George Zimmerman's lies. Instead, all they could see was a Black kid who was supposedly "up to no good." To have a fair trial with what we call a jury of our peers, we need to make it a law that future jurors should be an equally mixed race of jurors that represent different ethnic groups, not just one dominant race. Sadly to say, the statement "up to no good" is how some whites see young Black kids today. Most of them are not bad kids but merely trying to find their way through life's struggles.

It's just like the Woodstock era when many young white teenage hippies experienced pot and committed crimes, which didn't make them thugs. They were simply finding their way through life; many of them went on to become businessmen, lawyers, and doctors, as well as local and state political leaders.

The point is, in these two cases, race/color played a significant role in both jury's decisions. Hopefully, one day we can live out the profound words of Dr. Martin Luther King: "I have a dream that my four little children will one day live in a nation where they will not be judged by the color of their skin, but by the content of their character."

So, I ask that we all stop casting judgment on one another based on skin color and nationality. I believe everyone would agree that if this jury was predominately Black, George Zimmerman would have been locked up and served time for murder, and not just because they were a Black jury, but because he is guilty. Now, if I had been on both juries, I would have voted guilty for both Zimmerman and O. J. Simpson. However, in the case of the wonderful gentleman, Mr. Ahmaud Arbery, it looks like we are finally making some progress after a predominantly white jury, one Black and eleven Whites, found three White men guilty in a senseless murder of Mr. Arbery, a so-called suspicious Black jogger, jogging in a predominantly white neighborhood. This time the jury got it right; it's heartbreaking for minorities when we often find ourselves having to fiercely petition the legal system to receive something we should automatically get, which is our fundamental rights to a fair trial. I pray that this case sets the tone for future cases that when you are wrong, you are wrong despite your color. This is the picture that Lady Justice is supposed to portray with impartial judgment. The blindfold over her eyes represents impartial judgment; unfortunately, for too long and in too many cases, Lady Justice only had one eye covered. Moving forward, I trust and hope that we can convince her to cover both eyes, meaning that we, as Americans, still have much work to do to receive justice for all.

I can honestly say I don't see color when it comes to choosing between right or wrong. If you're wrong, you're wrong.

From reading previous chapters of this book, I'm sure you know by now I am not biased. It's a fact that race does play a role in our day-to-day decision-making, racism and discrimination have many faces, and we sometimes subconsciously discriminate. There are certain things we do or say that are mild forms of discrimination.

Discrimination has been a serious problem due to the lack of diversity in high places in our society; race and gender discrimination still hold places in "some," not all, institutions and structured organizations. Institutional and systematic racism exists in America, whether some whites see racism in America as a significant problem or not; unfortunately, some people don't believe that institutional and systematic racism exists at all. To them, I say you are out of touch and have lived in your own small, secluded world too long. Even though we have some institutional and systematic racism, that does not mean that America is a racist country because America is not a racist country.

If I had to categorize it, I would use three types of discrimination.

There is individual discrimination, which describes one's behavior as having the ability to affect or harm another individual of a different race, gender, or ethnic group. Then there's institutional discrimination, which is different because it refers to the policies of the dominant race of individuals who control these institutions. These are individuals who implement policies intended to have certain stipulations that affect unwanted groups. Finally, there is structural discrimination, which refers to the policy of a dominant race set in place to control these structural institutions with the intent to keep out different races, genders, and groups. Structural racism is also cultural, which exists all around our everyday lives, providing the normalization and replication of racism. This provides the foundation for white dominance in this country, whether intentional or unintentional.

In an effort to try to curb racism, we have created reverse discrimination in many cases, such as Affirmative Action, which is sometimes used to determine college admission, that inadvertently discriminates against white Americans. This is like a double-edged sword, even though minorities are at a greater disadvantage, especially Native Americans. That's why we need a system that's fair to all. On the other hand, it's easy to sit back and downplay the problem when you're born privileged, which is by no means something to be ashamed of; it's due to the foundation and structure of the arrival of the European people. White people share the privilege of being more widely accepted more than any other nationality in America. If you are Latino, African American, Mexican, or Arab, you're not going to receive the same preferential treatment when you walk into an upscale department store in some cases, or, in the case of the legal system, you may not receive the benefit of the doubt, even though we have come a long way with the idea of inclusion for all. That's just how it is.

Some white Americans can't see it because they never had the minority experience that we deal with from day to day. In the 1964 movie *Black Like Me*, John H. Griffin, a white man who used chemicals to change his skin color from white to Black, moved down south to conduct a race study. He found out quickly that it was a white man's world back then. Of course, the country has rapidly changed since then, again as we ushered in the idea of inclusion. We are a more diverse country, and people are more open to various ethnic groups. Still, there are some groups we discriminate against with subtle, hidden racism. Examples include discrimination against fat people, short people, the elderly, people not considered attractive, and Jews. It's sad to see that anti-Semitic crime against our dear Jewish brothers and sisters is on the rise. Therefore, we should stand with them in unity. Even our Mexican brothers and sisters are under attack, especially the Dreamers, who should be able to live in America with the goal of working toward obtaining citizenship and from there, moving forward with enforcing our immigration laws. The saddest of all is the discrimination against the mentally ill. They are hidden in the shadows of society. We moved them from the asylums where they were warehoused in mental homes and institutions, on to the streets, called Skid Row, and finally into prisons, to be medicated and forgotten, which is sad. But thanks be to God, we as a country have come a long way from the Jim Crow laws of exclusion to inclusion. However, there's more healing and work to be done.

    I challenge those in the African American community to do their part to put an end to the negative labels that are directed toward you. It would help if you considered ditching the saggy pants, which portray a bad boy look. Stop accepting scripts in Hollywood that reinforce negative stereotypes. Instead, choose positive roles. And please stop using the N-word toward each other. It is ludicrous to expect someone to respect you when you don't respect yourself. I could never understand how you could call one another the N-word and seriously not expect anyone else to call you the N-word. I would like to stress to the African American community and rap industry that using the N-word is not cool but degrading to one another, as former slave masters used it to mentally degrade our people. Using the N-word sets us back, characteristically and mentally, hundreds of years of progress. If you constantly call someone something, they and others may eventually believe it. Wake up, people: you are much brighter and better than that. I believe once you start valuing yourself and one another, other races will value you as well.

Just for the record, African Americans make up approximately 13% of the U.S. population. I resent the way we are viewed because of a few lawless African Americans, which may be around 2% of the total African American population. It's not fair to cast a dark shadow over the other 11%, who play by the rules, who are hardworking and family-oriented. I refuse to mention the lie about work ethics of Black people, that they are lazy and don't want to work. Blacks are hardworking people. Young Blacks hold most of the minimum wage and menial jobs. When driving up to a fast-food restaurant window, guess who will stick their head out the window? You got it: an African American. When I look back at all the accomplishments, achievements, and advancements we have made as descendants of slaves; I am very proud of my people and proud to be an American.

Now I will turn toward our nationwide police conflict that's been so prevalent in the media. We all know that, in many instances, African Americans do not get equal treatment when confronted or stopped by a policeman. I, for one, can say I have never been mistreated by a police officer after being stopped on a few occasions for minor traffic violations. Whenever an officer has approached me, he has always greeted me with respect, and I, in return, greeted him with respect and cooperated. I personally never see a cop as a bad guy who's picking on a Black man. I simply believe the officer is doing his job. I think everyone should see it that way. But there are times when cops don't play by the book; some racially profile certain ethnic groups and wrongfully charge them. These are thug cops who should not be protected by the so-called brotherhood but reported and removed from the department. All it takes is a few bad cops to make the good cops look bad, just as it takes a few thuggish Blacks to make the Black communities look bad.

I thank God for all the men and women in blue who put their lives on the line every day for American citizens and who often put themselves in harm's way in bad neighborhoods to intervene in Black-on-Black crime. These are the same precious, brave cops that some liberal groups are calling for defunding the police, which is not the answer; there are ways to help keep the bad cops in check without penalizing the good cops. I believe that some African American and Latino communities and police departments need to fill the gap of mistrust by building a bridge of communication with one another and getting to know each other in a positive way. They should take a more cooperative, community-oriented approach to bridging this gap. This would help weed out the bad guys, who are creating some of the problems within these communities. Also, as I shared previously, a lack of opportunities and desperation breed crime, which is no excuse, but it is a reality. Instead of society fixing the problem, we make the situation worse by locking them up in privatized prisons, where owners get to fatten their pockets through exploitation of cheap labor, providing little to no rehabilitation. This is a system that can possibly profile you, and prosecute you, for prisons for profit. After five years of being incarcerated around veteran con artists, a first-time criminal offender becomes worse than they were prior to being locked up. It doesn't take a rocket scientist to see that education, skills, job training, and teaching responsibility are far cheaper than incarceration. Plus, in the long run, we will create law-abiding, taxpaying citizens.

It will be a great period in the world if mankind can come to the point where the color of one's skin really doesn't matter.

It has been asked, what color was Jesus? Why does it matter? Especially when His teachings and laws are not partial but good and peaceful—like "love your enemies," "Therefore if thine enemy hunger, feed him," and "Thou shalt love thy neighbor as thyself." With teachings like this, it doesn't matter what color He is; I would follow this man to the end of the world and back without even a question.

I've seen Him portrayed as white, black, tan, brown, even multiple colors. These are nothing but false idols of Christ. As I stated earlier, it doesn't matter what color He is, as long as He loves all of us. And this is the same message we all should have: that it doesn't matter what color anyone is. We should love everyone, even as Christ loves us.

I believe America has far more good people than bad. I believe there are many people who truly would like to see America unite as one and not divided along racial lines. Dr. Martin Luther King Jr. once profoundly stated that 11 a.m. Sunday morning is "the most segregated hour in this nation." This remains a tragedy to this day for many Christian believers. There is no reason why we should be the most laughed-at country in the world when it comes to living out the decree democracy stands for. The word is out that America does not practice what it preaches when it comes to democracy. This belief is based on our preference for liberties and justice for all. Many countries would like to know who we are to scold them about human rights, while many people's rights are being violated here. This international mockery should inspire us to stand together and live out the decree of our Founding Fathers from the Declaration of Independence:

"We hold these truths to be self-evident, that all men are created equal, that they are endowed by their Creator with certain unalienable Rights, that among these are Life, Liberty and the pursuit of Happiness—That to secure these rights, Governments are instituted among Men, deriving their just powers from the consent of the governed—That whenever any Form of Government becomes destructive of these ends, it is the Right of the People to alter or to abolish it, and to institute new Government, laying its foundation on such principles and organizing its powers in such form, as to them shall seem most likely to affect their Safety and Happiness."

This writing is so powerful that it sends chills through my body whenever I read it. These words were written to govern this great country. If America remains divided racially, economically, and socially, she will never fulfill her full potential of being a greater nation. So, I say unto you, wherever you find injustice or racism trying to rear its ugly head and spread its venomous tentacles, cut it off with the sword of peace, whether it occurs in the workplace, school, armed forces, or even in your neighborhood. Let it be known it has no place here. Remember one thing about the devil: once you see him, you'll never forget him. What the world witnessed in Charlottesville, Virginia, on August 12, 2017, was pure evil—the devil himself. Sadly, to say, a precious young lady lost her life during a peaceful demonstration, speaking out against the evil of racism. I pray that God would open the eyes of the white racist to see that hatred is of the devil and convert all the negative energy of hate into the positive energy of love and of peace, and help make the world a better place for all mankind to live in. Racism and hatred remind me of a famous quote by

Nelson Mandela: "Resentment is like drinking poison and then hoping it will kill your enemies." We are not born to hate; we are taught to hate, so naturally, we can learn to love. Nelson Mandela spent twenty-seven years in South Africa as an apartheid political prisoner for fighting inequity and racism; of all people, he should have had a reason to hate; instead, he chose to forgive and love his fellow man. With the help of God, I intend to run a campaign that promotes Healing, Unity, and Opportunities for all Americans, not just minorities.

Now, concerning the history of minorities, it is not fair to say, "it's the past; just suck it up and get over it." I think there should always be a place and time to have open dialogues so people can discuss their past struggles that divided us and learn from our past, so history won't repeat itself. So, we can move forward to a better and brighter future. It would be insensitive to ask the Jewish community to stop whining and complaining about the Holocaust and move on with life, as well as asking the Native Americans to get over the Trail of Tears era, plus the ongoing injustice and disrespect as pipelines were run through their sacred burial grounds.

I think there is a lack of empathy in our country for a lot of people that received serious inhumane treatment. I think all Americans need to take a step back and stop blaming each other for our problems. And work toward showing unity, empathy, and concern for each other's situation, that we may pull together and make the country a better place for future generations.

The game of blaming people has wreaked havoc on the Asian American community, who have been blamed for COVID-19, followed by unfortunate brutal nationwide assaults on the American Asian communities. No one deserves this type of treatment; this is nothing but racism, and America feels your pain, and we stand in solidarity with you. As a reminder, we all live in this great country, so why not live in harmony? Since we are on this subject, I would like to address the relationship between the Asian and the Black communities. For years, the conversation among Black people concerning the treatment and attitude of Asian Americans shown toward the Black community is, they treat us like we are inferior to them and second-class citizens. However, on the contrary, the Whites are treated better. When a White person goes into their place of business, the Asians bow and smile and grin from ear to ear with royal treatment. However, most of the time, when a Black person goes in their business to patronize them, there are little to no smiles, no warm welcoming nor conversations, just distant cold feelings and little to no appreciation for patronizing their business. One of the biggest problems African Americans have with the Asian community, as commonly reported among each other, is the feeling of being watched and prejudged as though every Black person that comes into their business is going to steal something, which equals prejudice. For these reasons, Asian businesses are losing a lot of potential Black customers, who refuse to patronize and subject themselves to this type of environment. The general feeling of the Black community is Asians need to learn how to be more respectful and genuinely treat everybody equally. One of the greatest universal ideologies is, "to receive respect, one must show respect," sincerely shared in love.

    Racism mostly exists due to ignorance and fear of the unknown. To resolve it, we must let our guards down and get to know one another. *"To make a friend, you must first be willing to make an investment in a stranger"* (R. S. Porter). Who's ready to invest with me and change America with one smile and good deed at a time?

Let's go spread the message of love and peace and become race bridge-builders. God bless America!

In Conclusion

Racism. How does God feel about racism? Racism has been an ongoing problem throughout the ages in the Bible; we find many examples of feuds caused by racism in the Bible, especially concerning the Jews and the Gentiles. The Gentiles were considered heathens, and they were not accepted by Jewish people. To say the least, it was a strong hate-filled relationship. Jesus sums it all up in this scripture:

> *Jesus said unto him, Thou shalt love the Lord thy God with all thy heart, and with all thy soul, and with all thy mind. This is the first and great commandment. And the second is like unto it, Thou shalt love thy neighbour as thyself.*
>
> Matthew 22:37–39

Meaning, put yourself in their shoes and ask yourself the question, if I were in the same situation, how would I like to be treated? So, please let this be your approach to racism, and the world will be a better place. God bless you!

CHAPTER SIX
POLITICS

It has been said the word "politics" is derived from "poly," meaning "many," and "tics," meaning "blood-sucking parasites."

Now, let's dig into this subject! When it comes down to politics, the American people, and especially the church, have been greatly deceived. The church has allowed the IRS to put it to silence when it comes to politics out of fear of losing its nonprofit status. I believe in respecting the law, at least until it conflicts with God's law. Politics should never conflict with one's faith if the government understands what politics is really about. Here again, I believe in giving credit where credit's due. Thank God for former President Trump standing up for religious freedoms. His administration rewrote a bill that had preachers tongue-tied, called the Johnson Amendment. In its rewritten form, it allows Christians to speak freely about biblical and social issues that are prevalent in today's world. The bill does not repeal the Johnson Amendment. Instead, it amends the law to allow for free speech that is made "in the ordinary course of the organization's regular and customary activities." This is to say that, as you carry out the mission of your church or organization, you would have the right to speak freely on all issues of life, including candidates and elections. You would not have to fear IRS censorship or punishment for simply exercising your right to free speech and freedom of religion. Putting it in layman's terms, the bill inserts a legal clause for free speech into the Johnson Amendment that thankfully gets the IRS out of the business of policing the free speech of America's pastors and churches. This law allows us to be whistleblowers as we should be, speaking out when we see something that is not right.

So, what is politics?

Politics are the activities associated with the governance of a country. This is particularly regarding the debate among individuals or parties having or hoping to achieve power. In layman's terms, politics refers to people who come together, using a systemic way to vote for an individual or group with like-minded beliefs, to write laws on how to run their entity, city, state, or country. The majority population empowers these few people to represent them as their leaders. In this way, everyone must live by the laws that the group believes are in the best interest of the people, whether they are right or wrong, good or evil. Clergymen and Christians not only have a right to stand up and blow the whistle on a politician who tries to pass laws contrary to the Word of God, but we are obligated to expose the individual or group seeking to empower themselves so they can run your city, county, state, or country the way they want. Just as a warning: according to Proverbs, when the ungodly are in charge, all hell will break loose because the wicked have no fear of God and will legislate laws that are perverted and harmful to the righteous. Proverbs 29:2 says, *"When the righteous are in authority, the people rejoice: but when the wicked beareth rule, the people mourn."*

One of the saddest things I have ever heard is when a preacher says, "I don't get involved with politics." Why not politics? It's just a system we use to establish rules that govern the land. If the church and the righteous people of God do not get in the business of rulemaking for the country, one day, you might wake up and find a padlock on your church door with a letter stating: "This site is prohibited from unlawful assembly to teach the Bible; persons can congregate only to teach secular humanism and government-sanctioned material." This could happen because some individual or group believes there is no God, or they are anti-God. If the church doesn't wake up, this law could be coming to a neighborhood near you soon. As Edmund Burke profoundly stated, "The only thing necessary for the triumph of evil is for good men to do nothing." Therefore, I would like to encourage my fellow Americans to vote for just, righteous leaders who fear God. I believe that most of the country has been known to vote with their wallet and not their conscience. Stop selling out and stand on God's Word.

Today's politics are not much different than they were back in the 1930s. In 1931, the city of Chicago was run by the Golden Rule: "He that has the gold makes the rules." Those were the days of Prohibition when Al Capone bought both the city and its prominent politicians. He spent $75 million to control the city for his thuggish business ventures, which have been glamorized by so many people to this day. Just as it was back then, even now we see lobbyists and special interest groups buying power to influence decisions made by officials in government, mostly legislators or members of regulatory agencies.

Now, people of faith, can't you see why the devil doesn't want you to get involved? It's so he can run the show.

Furthermore, our political system is broken. We all have seen it repeated in Washington; politicians are so divided and stubborn that they can't even pass a bill together to prevent a government shutdown. If you ask me, it's time to send these lifelong politicians home and send a strong message to the big-name dynasty, left-wing politicians. This message would say, "Thanks for your service, but no thanks. We've had enough of you." It's time to move our country forward. It's time for a new day of politics with strong, godly politicians who will look out for all the American people, not just for the elitist, but for the rich and the poor, red and yellow, Black and White. We are all precious in God's sight. Most of these politicians only look out for themselves.

I believe in giving credit where credit is due. I applaud former President Obama for standing up for the people who could not afford medical insurance. By initiating The Affordable Care Act, this policy has saved the lives of many people who otherwise would be dead if our previous healthcare system was still in place. Many people were denied coverage in the past due to pre-existing conditions. The Affordable Care Act plan might not be the best plan, but it's better than nothing at all. The people who play a role in the regulatory field of medical care costs need to get the cost reduced, so everyone can afford it on their own, without relying on government subsidies. Only then should we discuss getting rid of the ACA. For those in Washington who need a reality check, there are millions of Americans who still can't afford health insurance. The cost for insurance coverage for a family of four is around $1,500–$3,000 per month, depending on your health conditions and your plan. Before the ACA, if you were in bad health, something as simple as high blood pressure would cause a higher increase in premiums.

It doesn't take a genius to figure out that medical insurance is unaffordable for people earning minimum wage. I hear the Republicans blistering about repealing Obamacare, which is fine. Unfortunately, the question is, what do you intend to use in order to replace it? I don't think they know just how many people it will hurt or possibly kill; whatever healthcare plan they come up with, make sure it shows more empathy toward the poor, so they can receive affordable proper healthcare. When it comes to healthcare for the poor, money shouldn't be an issue; just simply look out for the American people...end of story!

The Republicans act as though all poor people want government hand-outs. At the same time, none of them had rolled out a plan for healthcare, only shown smokescreens and talk. It's like, "I got mine, and you get yours." I mean, some politicians are out of touch with the heartbeat and pulse of the American people. These politicians have the best medical coverage that money can buy. It's time to stop playing politics with people's lives; I encourage the Republican Party to stop acting like everybody is lazy and just wants government handouts, and it's your personal money. When you step up to the plate and show empathy for the American people, especially during a national crisis such as a pandemic, people will respect you and never forget how you were there when they needed you the most, and they will be willing to support you and make sacrifices for the country if the country ever needs them.

There have been election terms when I voted Republican. Then there were terms when I didn't vote at all because there was no one I felt led by God for whom to vote. We had Mitt Romney, who seemed to have been against supporting the 47% who supposedly don't pay taxes and receive government subsidies. Instead, he was strongly in favor of the elitists. And we had Barack Obama, whose moral beliefs were totally opposite of mine. Examples included same-sex marriage and abortion; as a result, my faith wouldn't allow me to vote for him. I am sure someone would argue why I wouldn't vote for the lesser of two evils. My answer is that I refuse to ever compromise with my faith and the Word of God. It doesn't matter who you are, what color you are, or what you offer me; I refuse to empower anyone to pass laws that promote evil doing. As a Christian, once you learn about a person's beliefs, if they don't line up with God's Word, you shouldn't vote for them. To vote for someone whose beliefs do not line up with the Word of God makes you just as guilty as they are because you are aiding and supporting them. Unfortunately, the candidates who ran in the 2016 presidential race were not that impressive. Some of the televised presidential debates were seen as immature and very un-presidential. There was one presidential candidate that I have great respect for: that's the late great honorable Senator John McCain, a man of integrity. I will never forget when one of his supporters in a town hall meeting called then-Senator Barack Obama an Arab; McCain then cut the woman off and took back the microphone. "No, ma'am," he said. "He's a decent family man [and a] citizen that I just happen to have disagreements with on fundamental issues, and that's what the campaign's all about. He's not [an Arab]. Thank you." John McCain stopped her and defended his opponent with such grace and integrity; this is a rarity in today's politics. To me, this man is more than a war hero; he is an example to our country as far as what it is to be patriotic and how he served our country with dignity and grace. What a sad loss of a wonderful human being and a great American politician. God bless him. Rest in peace.

To the African American community, I would like to share some things that you may not be in knowledge of concerning the Democrat Party. For starters, the Democrat Party has become very anti-God, and they are in cahoots with the cancel culture organizations and companies that will try to destroy you if you do not believe in the same immoral ideology that they embrace.

If you do not "kiss the Ring" and accept their belief system, they will seek to cancel you out of mainstream society. Well, guess what? Whatever is not of God, I will never accept, and you can't cancel me out; I cancel you out because my God, whom I serve, holds all power and final authority. To cancel me out, you have to cancel God out, and you know that will never happen. As a warning to the African American communities, before you vote again for the Democrat Party, make sure you know and understand what the Democrat Party stands for and what it promotes that God hates. They support the following:

1) Late-term abortion.
2) Loose voter ID laws that can lead to voter fraud.
3) Transgender sex change in the military.
4) Same-sex marriage.
5) Intentional open border policy that allows undocumented immigrants to enter the United States; they will eventually give them voting rights to help win future elections.
6) Not committed to supporting Israel 100%.
7) Allowing a thirteen-year-old child to consent to gender reassignment (sex change) without parental approval, which takes control away from the parents on a major mutilation change that cannot be reversed. Your child is not EVEN allowed to participate in after-school sports or extra-curricular activities without the written consent of adult parents or guardians. See how ridiculous this policy is?
8) And last but not least, opposition to freedom of religion and freedom of speech. The Democrat Party is trying to stop preachers from preaching in the name of Jesus and mandate that we should accept and embrace

all forms of religions.

In Conclusion

Politics. As a Christian, please don't be afraid to stand up and speak out against immorality and injustice. Don't be intimidated or pressured to vote for something you know deep down inside is wrong. Please get involved in politics, which is the act of making laws for you and your children's children to live by for generations to come. As a warning, never vote for any politician who does not support Israel and her right to exist as a State. I believe the U.S. should stand by Israel at all costs. So, vote for godly men and not your wallet, and always remember that your vote counts.

CHAPTER SEVEN
FAITH AND RELIGION IN AMERICA

Faith is one of the biggest issues dividing America. This is one of those taboo subjects that folks rarely like to talk about. We all know the unwritten rules of the workplace: Don't discuss religion, politics, and sports. Why not? As adults, we should be able to discuss anything; in the end, we can either agree or disagree. But we can still agree to respect each other as human beings and peacefully agree to disagree. So, let's talk!

Why is the subject of faith so taboo? I believe the reason we shun the subject of faith is because of our fear of being rejected, offended, ignored, or embarrassed about the religion we were raised in, which leads to feelings of indifference.

What is religion? It's an organized collection of beliefs, cultural systems, and world views that relate to humanity, spirituality, and the supernatural. Many religions may have organized behaviors, clergy, and a definition of what constitutes membership. Religions often feature holy places, ritual commemorations, deity worship, festivals, dances, even mythology worship, and so on.

Now this explains why people avoid talking about their beliefs. It's because they have religion, yet they do not have FAITH! Faith in Jesus Christ, the Son of God. There are some who say there is no God; Psalm 14:1–2 states:

> *The fool hath said in his heart, There is no God. They are corrupt, they have done abominable works, there is none*

that doeth good. The LORD looked down from heaven upon the children of men, to see if there were any that did understand, and seek God.

Some claim that man evolved from a primate, citing human evolution. However, the book of Genesis 1:24–25 says this:

And God said, Let the earth bring forth the living creature after his kind, cattle, and creeping thing, and beast of the earth after his kind: and it was so. And God made the beast of the earth after his kind, and cattle after their kind, and every thing that creepeth upon the earth after his kind: and God saw that it was good.

In this record of creation, it included primates, so God made primates; they did not evolve. Then, after He made the animals, you will find in Genesis 1:26–27 that He made man:

And God said, Let us make man in our image, after our likeness: and let them have dominion over the fish of the sea, and over the fowl of the air, and over the cattle, and over all the earth, and over every creeping thing that creepeth upon the earth. So God created man in his own image, in the image of God created he him; male and female created he them. And the LORD God formed man of the dust of the ground, and breathed into his nostrils the breath of life; and man became a living soul.

Genesis 2:7

As you can clearly see, God made two distinct creations: man and animals. This alone should kill the theory of evolution. And if not, here's the million-dollar question: Why don't the other apes and monkeys drop their tails and come down out of the trees and walk upright? I know if I were a primate living in a jungle and had the opportunity to make the change, I would make the change in a heartbeat. I mean, really, *come on!* Who wouldn't take a townhouse over a treehouse? If a man is just a bunch of sophisticated apes, I'll put my Bible down and never preach again. Because that would mean the Bible isn't true, and I would feel like the Apostle Paul when he says the following:

> *Now if Christ be preached that he rose from the dead, how say some among you that there is no resurrection of the dead? But if there be no resurrection of the dead, then is Christ not risen: And if Christ be not risen, then is our preaching vain, and your faith is also vain. Yea, and we are found false witnesses of God; because we have testified of God that he raised up Christ: whom he raised not up, if so be that the dead rise not. For if the dead rise not, then is not Christ raised: And if Christ be not raised, your faith is vain; ye are yet in your sins. Then they also which are fallen asleep in Christ are perished. If in this life only we have hope in Christ, we are of all men most miserable.*
>
> 1 Corinthians 15:12–19

So, therefore, if we evolved from primates, then the Bible is not true, and our preaching is in vain, meaning we have no hope for eternal life after death. Now, if this is the case, I would feel like Apostle Paul, most miserable, if there is no hope of a future resurrection for the Saints of God after we die. But, as Christians, we know the Bible is true, and that God made man in His image, and that Jesus Christ rose from the dead, and so shall we rise from the grave one day to be with Him in heaven.

Someone has asked the question, what is Christianity? It's the opposite of religion; it's faith in God through Jesus Christ, simply a way of life. It is these things rather than a religious belief system of rituals. As Christians, we are able to live a life of victory and peace by possessing the fruit of the Spirit. Consider Galatians 5:22–23:

> *But the fruit of the Spirit is love, joy, peace, longsuffering, gentleness, goodness, faith, Meekness, temperance: against such there is no law.*

In addition, Ephesians 2:8–9 states:

> *For by grace are ye saved through faith; and that not of yourselves: it is the gift of God: Not of works, lest any man should boast.*

We are saved by grace, for it is the gift of God through His Son Jesus, being justified by faith, repentance, and believing that Jesus died on the cross and was resurrected on the third day. This part of the faith is what gives us the ability to receive salvation. You also will receive power to overcome sin, to walk as a new creature after being baptized in water, in the name of Jesus Christ for the remission of sins, and receiving the precious gift of the Holy Ghost by the evidence of speaking in tongues, as the Spirit gives you utterance. This gives us power to live right, walk right, talk right, and love right. It gives us the power to overcome all habit-forming vices, such as drugs, alcohol, porn, sexual sin, and such things that Satan throws at you, which the blood of Jesus has already defeated.

Now that I have laid my foundation on religion, faith, and the tenets of Christianity, almost everyone in the world knows that America is a nation built upon Christianity. This is who we are. Why do we feel that we should be silent about it? This is especially true about the message of the cross and how the Son of God, who was born of a virgin named Mary, gave His life on the cross and shed His blood for all men that we may have eternal life. Since this is who we are and what we believe, why have we dismissed prayer in public schools and removed Bibles from schools? And one of the most unforgettable attacks on America's faith was when the country sat back and allowed one lone, rogue federal judge in Montgomery, Alabama, to order the removal of a 2.6-ton granite monument of the Ten Commandments from the courthouse, citing separation of Church and State. You can't separate the Church from the state because the Church makes up the State and vice versa. What a joke! The Church and the State are one because some of the lawmakers attend Church and share the same beliefs. The Founding Fathers of this great nation would be appalled if they could revisit us.

The liberals are trying to take away what I love about this country the most: its foundation rests upon the Holy Word of God. If we take away God's Word, we have no foundation. We cannot afford to sit back and allow a few evil-hearted, blind judges and lawmakers to divide the country on issues we know deep in our hearts are right. They're destroying the country's foundation in the name of so-called unconstitutional. This is nothing but liberalism at its best; it's a plot to try to get rid of God. If the liberals can take God out of the picture, they won't have to answer to anyone. If there's no God, there's no right or wrong, meaning no more moral restraints, which means anything and everything goes.

Here's one of the devil's tricks that politicians use to get into office: they don't reveal their true plans and beliefs until they get elected. If we have more Christians with conservative values, how then did these liberals get into office? They are wolves in disguise who come to you in sheep's clothing. We, as Christians, must be prayerful about who we vote for. There were election terms I could not vote and live with a clear conscience, knowing both individual candidates' beliefs did not line up with my Christian values and what their administrations stood for. So, what do we do? Choose between the lesser of the two evils.

Some preacher friends and acquaintances of mine couldn't understand why I wouldn't help make history by voting for a Black man. I shared with them that, first, I had been following the campaign debates and wasn't pleased with Mr. Barack Obama's answers back when he was Senator Obama. I felt like there was a hidden agenda from the beginning of his campaign when he was questioned on certain moral issues. Many times, he avoided the question or answered indirectly on specific questions, such as abortion and same-sex marriage. These issues should be answered yay or nay, not shady gray. I believe when it comes to leading the free world, candidates running for office should make themselves clear and be candid in their moral beliefs. Secondly, I told them I couldn't vote for a man based solely on his skin color. That was exactly what most of the Black community had done. Don't get me wrong: I believe Mr. Barack Obama was just as qualified for the job as the next man. After all, he is very intelligent and has a heart to help everybody. But regardless, you can't please and help people when they ask you to support their evil deeds. A lot of Black pastors, leaders, and African Americans never saw it coming. They were shocked when he came out of the closet in favor of same-sex marriages. However, I wasn't. I saw it coming all along.

One thing about the African American community is that we are a people of high moral values. For example, 82% of the Black community is strongly against same-sex marriage.

We are traditionally faith-oriented, God-fearing people, not homophobic. I've heard many say, "If I had known this, I wouldn't have voted for him." The thing we all must remember is that kings, presidents, prime ministers, and leaders come and go. They all fade away along with their glory, but the Word of God endures forever. They are just mere mortal men who will return back to the dust: from out of the ground we were taken, and to the ground we shall return, from ashes to ashes and dust the dust. When they are long gone, our children's children will have to deal with mad laws that were implemented by them. But hopefully, one day, these laws will be overturned due to the fear of God. Therefore, we must restore our country back to biblical truths so that there are no inscribed laws that would bring God's wrath upon us.

So now, I ask the church—the sleeping giant; he that is supposed to be mighty, strong, and watchful—why sleep in the time of trouble? Know ye not that we are under attack? Have you not been appointed the keeper of the gate, of the city of our God, and the watchman of souls? It seems like many church leaders have forgotten our mission, which is to go into the world as a bright light, illuminating where there's darkness, liberating the captive from the power of darkness, and bringing them to the light that they may bear much fruit for Christ Jesus.

Instead, many of the televangelists' ministries are like drug dealers and panhandlers, peddling off their spiritual, quick-fix, get-high, feel-good materials like books, CDs, vials of oil, and so-called holy water. They are like modern-day snake oil salesmen who use their classic sales pitches at the end of a broadcast. "Don't miss out on your blessing. For only $99, I'll show you how to receive your healing, how to obtain deliverance from satanic power, and how to receive the baptism of the Holy Ghost." And don't forget the classic "seven keys to prosperity." It's like you must pay before you can receive help. Even doctors aren't that bad; at least they treat you and bill you later. With ministries nowadays, it's like you can't receive my divine revelation from God until you pay me; sometimes, to make themselves feel good, they will occasionally send you a freebie, mainly to put you in their contact list for future solicitation. Sometimes they require you to purchase a ticket online or pay at the door to get into their services, to so-called "hear the gospel." Jesus said: *"Freely ye have received, freely give."* These practices are a disgrace to the gospel. It has gone too far; it's like prostitution of God's Word. It's a turn-off to the secular world. I would like to apologize to all who have been offended. I ask you to please forgive us because the things you're seeing aren't what the true Church stands for.

I understand that it takes money to operate ministries; therefore, to offer certain material gifts to one's partners is fine for their monetary support. And even to challenge or teach one to give is fine. The Word of God encourages us to give and to sow monetary seeds. Luke 6:38 declares:

> *Give, and it shall be given unto you; good measure, pressed down, and shaken together, and running over, shall men give into your bosom. For with the same measure that ye mete withal it shall be measured to you again.*

God also commands the rich to communicate with their wealth, which means to give of their resources.

> *Charge them that are rich in this world, that they be not highminded, nor trust in uncertain riches, but in the living God, who giveth us richly all things to enjoy; That they do good, that they be rich in good works, ready to distribute, willing to communicate;*
>
> 1 Timothy 6:17–18

However, the gimmick of asking someone to send you an offering in order for God to get their son out of jail or to cure their daughter of cancer is pure manipulation and deceiving. Jesus Christ has already paid the price for our healing. Again, if you charge people a fee to get into your service before they can hear the gospel means you are blind and marginalize certain people who can't afford $30 to $270 to get in the arena and sit in choice seats and by no means is it biblically acceptable. Someone asked the question, "What Would Jesus Do?" (WWJD?) Mind you, there's a lot I don't know about The Lord, but one thing I do know: He wouldn't charge a soul one red penny to get into a facility to hear the gospel of salvation, and neither should you. A free-will offering should suffice unless you are trying to build your own personal financial portfolio off the gospel. I believe you should preach the Word and what's right; God will pay, whether you receive it in this life or the next life. This is not the time to seek riches and wealth, but souls for the Glory of God's kingdom. There appears to be more focus on the money than the mission of soul-saving. There have been these reality TV shows in the past about preachers of LA, Detroit, and Atlanta. It's like an inside look at their lives and a behind-the-scenes look at a pastor's ministries; we're not called to expose the church's adversities and failures to the secular world.

It shows pastors showing off their bling-bling and flaunting their prosperity. It's like the blind leading the blind. There's nothing wrong with being successful as a preacher. God's Word promotes prosperity and success. Nevertheless, I truly believe that the church has gone overboard concerning materialistic possessions; this message can occasionally hurt the church's credibility.

Money should be used as a tool to help create opportunities for people, like helping third-world countries, feeding and housing the poor, and spreading the gospel. I can't see how a pastor can take church funds and buy a half-million-dollar car just to ride around in, while his members are struggling from day to day to make ends meet. What's my point? Jesus rode a donkey to preach the gospel. It makes you wonder about the mindset of some of these preachers, especially when many churchgoers can hardly pay their rent, and some must even choose between medication or food.

It's not always wrong for a pastor to own a jet or nice cars to make his job easier; we do represent the kingdom of God and the Bible depicts heaven as a place of riches, having streets made of gold. However, I challenge pastors to get back to the mission of soul-saving and preach the raw, uncompromising, unadulterated Word of God for His glory. I challenge pastors to put an end to this pie-in-the-sky, happy-go-lucky prosperity religion, and going through the motions of ceremonies and rituals, going about building megastructures and calling it a church, but in some cases, it's just a giant country club. Many churches have forsaken the ideas of gathering in the name of the Lord to worship and calling upon the Lord with the purpose of hearing from heaven and invoking God's presence and manifestations of His Spirit. Is He in the midst of your gathering? No. Why? He isn't there because you never invited Him. He's not even on your resurrection program; instead of recognizing Christ on Resurrection Sunday, many churches will participate in what's called the church Easter Egg Hunt. The White House has a traditional Easter Egg Roll that allows little children to hunt for eggs, having lied to them that the Easter Bunny laid them. In retrospect, the White House should forbid such pagan practice and nonsense to be held in commemoration of Christ's Resurrection and instead allow the story of the cross to be displayed. The same nonsense ritual is practiced at Christian churches throughout the world. This goes to show how Satan has incorporated this ungodly pagan tradition to be practiced in many churches even to this day, who continue to obscure the true message of the cross and how our Lord and Savior Jesus Christ suffered and died for the sins of the world.

Many Christians will gather in a solemn assembly on what we call Good Friday as many have been falsely taught to believe Christ died on Good Friday. Many will also go to church early on so-called Easter sunrise morning to commemorate His early resurrection. You cannot get three days and three nights from Friday evening to Sunday morning. The Bible said that Jesus was in the grave for three days and three nights. Here we can clearly see another misconception of our faith.

Wait, there's more. Talk about obscurity when it comes to Christmas. His name does not even appear on some of His birthday cards. Instead, it states Merry *"Xmas."* This is not saying one is trying to X out Christ, but aren't we watering down the message? He's not even invited to church for His own birthday celebration. And even if He were invited to church or the Christmas party for His birthday, He would probably go unnoticed because everybody's focus is on the decor, gifts, eating and drinking, and singing Christmas carols. Please don't forget about the center of attraction, the Christmas tree. We are usually more interested in the tree than He who hung and died on the tree. It's appalling that we have taken two sacred holidays and made them somewhat of a mockery.

Just because you don't take your faith seriously, that doesn't mean others don't. Some religions will not tolerate mockery or nonsense concerning their religion. We make light of our faith in so many ways that we're treading on the grounds of heresy in the church. The Muslims have much more regard for their holy days than we do, especially for those of us who know the truth of God's Word. This is a shame before God Almighty; this should bring you to tears. We think everything should have a joke attached to it, even if it's sacred. I've heard people make fun of other religions in the name of freedom of speech. That's not freedom of speech; it's mockery, disrespect, and recklessly irresponsible behavior in the name of freedom of speech. You can't win anyone to Christ this way, regardless of whether they are right or wrong; that's not Christ-like. Just because you don't take your faith seriously, that doesn't mean others don't. I challenge you to awaken and take your rightful place because we have the truth. We are not a religion, as you read earlier in this chapter. Religion could mean a lot of things regarding belief systems and many gods. We are not a religious nation; we are a God-fearing nation that serves the one and only true Righteous God. As a Christian, don't ever be ashamed of who you are. Instead, you should declare it from the rooftop, and this is my desire to proclaim the message in this book from the rooftop, the mountains tops, the valleys, and from coast to coast.

I've noticed during Christmas holidays that many businesses have trained their employees to wish you a "Happy Holiday," omitting the traditional greeting of "Merry Christmas" out of fear of offending others, citing political correctness. Some public schools even use the term "Winter Break" instead of "Christmas Break," and some states and local institutions have even omitted Christmas nativity scenes. However, there is a nativity scene of the baby Baphomet (Satan) that is displayed annually in the Illinois State Capitol Rotunda, which the Satanic Temple has deceived them into thinking it's unconstitutional not to allow them to display the nativity of the baby Satan alongside the traditional baby Jesus nativity scene. Now that's crazy! Please wake up, people.

Also, when it comes to Halloween, the devil's holiday, it's okay to express yourself; kids can come to school dressed as goblins, pirates, and vampires. Yes, it's celebrating Halloween, but you can't call it that; it's known as a costume day. They pass out treats but don't call it trick-or-treat. They can celebrate the day of the devil, but not the day honoring Christ.

Let's stop taking a backseat with your faith; it seems like we're afraid of expressing our true faith. Stop trying to be politically correct; instead, be God-correct. Our children can't pray out loud in school out of fear of other children or their parents who don't believe in Jesus Christ, so now, many can't pray out loud to God in fear of a lawsuit by a nonbeliever. But go to an Islamic country, enroll your child in their school system, and when they have prayer hours, try filing a complaint or getting a lawyer to sue the school because it offends your faith. You might be fortunate to escape with your head.

But anybody can come to America and tell you when to pray, how to pray, and what to pray. We can't pray at some graduations or sporting events. Oh, yeah, I forgot; the devil does allow you to have a moment of silence. I understand that America is a country of diversity. However, we should be able to practice our faith freely. Christ Jesus is simply who we are, and He was the foundation upon which this country was founded. America is a Christian nation, and we're deeply devoted to our faith in Jesus Christ. If we don't turn things around, I know the question that future generations of Christians will ask one another: What in the world were they thinking?

We need more men like the late Dr. Billy Graham, men full of integrity, humility, purity of heart, and the love of God. These are men who are not seeking wealth or power but rather who live a modest life. Dr. Graham had a big heart for ministry to see souls get saved. We saw him as a good example of a true man of God. Hats off to the many hard-working pastors who really love their ministry and show it by the devotion and passion they exemplify daily. Many of them make great sacrifices by sometimes putting the ministry before their personal and family needs to ensure the churches and the people's needs are met first. And they will give you the shirts off their backs; now, these are true men and women of God. My biggest reward in ministry, and I believe also with other pastors, is seeing God transform lives and save souls through their ministry.

I challenge the church to get back to the message of the cross, death, burial, resurrection of Jesus Christ, and the baptismal of the Holy Ghost that's given by the evidence of speaking in tongues, baptizing in the name of Jesus Christ for the remission of sins, and the saving power of God's grace.

We're not called to entertain the world; what the church needs to do is get on one accord because we're too divided along denominational lines. Of course, I know, realistically speaking, that all churches won't ever come together because of our differences in doctrine. However, for those who believe that Jesus Christ is the Son of God, born of a virgin, who died on the cross, was buried and rose from the grave on the third day to save the souls of mankind. We should be able to join hands in faith to achieve a common goal to stop the liberals and their ideology, which has the mindset of "do whatever you want to do…it's your prerogative…who cares what God thinks? I am my own man." We also need to come together and stop cancel-culture that's bent on silencing the church and stop anyone who threatens our Christian, godly values. My prayer is that all God-fearing churches will cross denominational lines, fight for the soul of America and create a nationwide movement of God with expectations of a revival. And push to put godly leaders in office to establish a godly decree in America. Please sign up at lyna.org and become a *Defender of The Faith* to take back America.

If you believe in Isaiah 7:14, we have some common ground to work together.

> *Therefore the Lord himself shall give you a sign; Behold, a virgin shall conceive, and bear a son, and shall call his name Immanuel.*

The name Immanuel means "God is with us." He came robed in the flesh and died on Calvary for the sins of mankind. He rose from the dead and ascended into heaven and gave gifts unto men, even the gift of the Holy Ghost. Here are the benefits of the gift of the Holy Ghost, according to Acts 2:17–18:

> *And it shall come to pass in the last days, saith God, I will pour out of my Spirit upon all flesh: and your sons and your daughters shall prophesy, and your young men shall see visions, and your old men shall dream dreams: And on my servants and on my handmaidens I will pour out in those days of my Spirit; and they shall prophesy.*

Through this same gift, God has shown me things that have come to pass and will come to pass. God said that He would show His people visions and dreams. Remember that, earlier in the book, I said I would tell you about a dream I had? Well, one day, the Lord showed me a powerful dream, a dream I'm compelled to share with the world as a warning. In my dream, I was standing on a riverbank in the Spirit, and there was a bear in the water feeding on the fish. I looked up and saw an eagle, which landed on top of the bear's shoulders as he stood upright. Out of anger, the bear took his front paw and struck the eagle, wounding it. So, the eagle flew off into the trees on the other side of the river. I immediately dove into the water to go see about the eagle, and as I looked around, I saw a woman in the water dressed in black. I began to swim toward her and noticed that I was swimming against the current with no problem, signifying the strength and anointing of God upon me. Once I reached her, I tried to help her out of the water, but she resisted my help. Then I looked and saw another woman coming out of the water dressed in white.

When I woke from the dream, I immediately knew it was from the Lord. So, for many days, I pondered it in my heart, and finally, the Lord revealed its meaning to me. The interpretation is that the bear and the eagle represent two nations; both have the same common interests since the bear and the eagle love fish. They fought over the same fishing spot, as will these two nations in the future.

They both love power, natural resources, and territories, and both are full of pride. Therefore, it is inevitable that one day they will clash. But the Lord will not be with the eagle because the bear has shown more regard for the Lord. The woman in black represents those who have rejected the Word of God and the admonishment and counsel of God's servants. The woman in black also represents those we have warned of the madness of aborting innocent unborn babies, passing laws to legalize the perversion of homosexuality and all the corruption in America. Still, you would not hear us as God's servants; therefore, your blood should be on your own hands. The woman in white represents those who are still standing for God. Not all have forsaken the Lord's Word. According to 1 King 19:13–18:

> *And it was so, when Elijah heard it, that he wrapped his face in his mantle, and went out, and stood in the entering in of the cave. And, behold, there came a voice unto him, and said, What doest thou here, Elijah? And he said, I have been very jealous for the LORD God of hosts: because the children of Israel have forsaken thy covenant, thrown down thine altars, and slain thy prophets with the sword; and I, even I only, am left; and they seek my life, to take it away. And the LORD said unto him, Go, return on thy way to the wilderness of Damascus: and when thou comest, anoint Hazael to be king over Syria: And Jehu the son of Nimshi shalt thou anoint to be king over Israel:*

and Elisha the son of Shaphat of Abelmeholah shalt thou anoint to be prophet in thy room. And it shall come to pass, that him that escapeth the sword of Hazael shall Jehu slay: and him that escapeth from the sword of Jehu shall Elisha slay. Yet I have left me seven thousand in Israel, all the knees which have not bowed unto Baal, and every mouth which hath not kissed him.

Notice verse 18 talks about a people who God had reserved in Israel, who did not follow the norm of pagan idol worship of that time but stood with God and His Word, regardless of the many threats for not participating in the pagan worship. There was also this one particular pagan god by the name of Moloch that the tribes of Israel served; during the time, the children of Israel turned away from God and worshiped Moloch. They even sacrificed their newborn babies on his altar. Those babies were burned to death with fire. It's the same thing today with abortion; parents sacrifice their babies to the god of pleasure and convenience.

So, thanks to God, who has reserved a people in America who have not bowed down to judicial, man-made, ungodly laws that oppose God's laws, which are supreme to all laws. We must trust and stand on God's Word, no matter what man says or how things look. We cannot afford to be like Sarah, Abraham's wife. She doubted God and created a big mess that affects us even to this day. Her disobedience to God is the reason Israel and the Arabs are fighting today. It has been said that religion has caused more wars than anything else. I don't know if that's true or not, but I do know there are warring factions that will never end, particularly the contentious, internal conflict between Israel and the Palestinians, known as the PLO, Palestine Liberation Organization. These two cultures will never be able to co-exist according to God's Holy Word.

That's why future Israeli prime ministers should never compromise with radical Muslims.

Let's take a glimpse into the truth behind this age-old conflict. The story goes like this: God had promised Sarah, Abraham's wife, who was barren, that He would open her womb and allow her to conceive a child in her old age. But as she grew older, she began to doubt God and gave her husband her handmaid servant to marry and to have a surrogate child for them. So, Abraham married Hagar, the Egyptian woman, and she had a child, naming him Ishmael. This child later had children who became mighty tribes. In modern days, they are called the Arabs. Now, once Hagar became pregnant, Sarah grew jealous and treated her cruelly and harshly, so the Egyptian woman ran away from Sarah. Here's how the story goes:

> *Now Sarai Abram's wife bare him no children: and she had an handmaid, an Egyptian, whose name was Hagar. And Sarai said unto Abram, Behold now, the LORD hath restrained me from bearing: I pray thee, go in unto my maid; it may be that I may obtain children by her. And Abram hearkened to the voice of Sarai. And Sarai Abram's wife took Hagar her maid the Egyptian, after Abram had dwelt ten years in the land of Canaan, and gave her to her husband Abram to be his wife. And he went in unto Hagar, and she conceived: and when she saw that she had conceived, her mistress was despised in her eyes. And Sarai said unto Abram, My wrong be upon thee: I have given my maid into thy bosom; and when she saw that she had conceived, I was despised in her eyes:*

the LORD judge between me and thee. But Abram said unto Sarai, Behold, thy maid is in thy hand; do to her as it pleaseth thee. And when Sarai dealt hardly with her, she fled from her face. And the angel of the LORD found her by a fountain of water in the wilderness, by the fountain in the way to Shur. And he said, Hagar, Sarai's maid, whence camest thou? and whither wilt thou go? And she said, I flee from the face of my mistress Sarai. And the angel of the LORD said unto her, Return to thy mistress, and submit thyself under her hands. And the angel of the LORD said unto her, I will multiply thy seed exceedingly, that it shall not be numbered for multitude. And the angel of the LORD said unto her, Behold, thou art with child, and shalt bear a son, and shalt call his name Ishmael; because the LORD hath heard thy affliction. And he will be a wild man; his hand will be against every man, and every man's hand against him; and he shall dwell in the presence of all his brethren.

Genesis 16:1–12

You'll notice Verse 12 says: *"And he will be a wild man; his hand will be against every man, and every man's hand against him; and he shall dwell in the presence of all his brethren."*

Does that not sound like radical Islam as we know it today? It should, because they are the children of the Egyptian woman, Hagar's son, Ishmael. History claims that Ishmael, son of Abraham, moved into the area we now call *Arabia*. It claims that the Arab people are the direct descendants of Ishmael. Muslims agree that this is true. They believe that the promised son of Abraham in Genesis is Ishmael, not Isaac. This means that they believe they are the rightful heirs over the land of Israel.

One of the biggest lessons we all should learn from this is that we should never doubt or disobey God's Word as an individual or as a country because it can bring years of grief, sorrow, and pain upon you, your family, and an entire nation.

As you can see, there's no end to this conflict. Even former President Bill Clinton tried to bring them together in 2000. The Camp David Summit peace talks with Israeli Prime Minister Ehud Barak and Palestinian leader Yasser Arafat came together, only to end in a three-hour elusive discussion that yielded no progress toward peace. Prime Minister Yitzhak Rabin even offered to give up land for peace, which later caused him to be considered a traitor. This is a no-no. The land of Israel should never be put on the table for negations of peace. Even former President Trump tried to establish peace deals with Arabic states, but for decades most Arabic states have boycotted Israel, insisting they would only establish ties after the Palestinian dispute was settled. Well, unfortunately, Palestinian and Israel disputes will never be settled; there will never be peace because of the prophetic Word you have read, until the return of the Prince of Peace Jesus Christ. The Word of God cannot be changed. They will live in the midst of each other but never be able to get along. This is why future Prime Ministers must take a stand, regardless of what world leaders say. Many world leaders opposed former President Trump's push to make Jerusalem the capital of Israel. The successor of Prime Minister Benjamin Netanyahu should never flinch under pressure when it comes to securing Israel's rights as an independent state. They must look out for the best interests of Israel and her right to exist because history has proven the Arab's intentions, which are to annihilate Israel. Unto the peaceful Muslim brothers and sisters, I hope after reading and understanding the truth behind this conflict, you will reassess your thoughts and allow God to lead you to the truth.

I believe that America has always been a Christian nation and still is, but I must confess that we are losing ground toward immorality and a lack of spirituality. What we need is a nationwide revival based on love, unity, and repentance toward God to make America a better place to live.

In my role as a Christian, rather than living a self-centered life, I encourage you to redeem the time, for the days are evil. Your life is too short to waste away on a self-centered life.

God says our life is like a vapor.

> *Go to now, ye that say, To day or to morrow we will go into such a city, and continue there a year, and buy and sell, and get gain: Whereas ye know not what shall be on the morrow. For what is your life? It is even a vapour, that appeareth for a little time, and then vanisheth away.*
>
> James 4:13–14

FINAL WORDS

This book is full of issues that we as Americans have our own opinions about; however, your opinions and my opinion do not count; only what God has spoken through His Word matters. Nevertheless, I feel as though I've given you true facts so you can make an educated choice on where you stand concerning these issues. Please remember: *A Divided Kingdom Cannot Stand*. America and the churches are too divided.

I believe there is great hope for the church of today if we stand up together as one and proclaim God's Word and stand our ground for Christ to build a greater America. We can achieve this by preaching love, unity, and repentance toward God and by spreading the message of love, peace, and hope.

So, wake up, thou sleeping Giant (the church), and be about your Father's business; the return of our Lord and Savior is near.

> "To me, the Bible is like a world compass; in it you will discover it's our light in the time of darkness, hope in the time of despair, and courage in time of fear. Without the Word of God, the world would be morally and eternally lost."
>
> R. S. Porter

I would like to encourage America to remain true to its roots as a God-fearing, caring, and generous nation. America is truly "the land of the free and the home of the brave." Thanks to God and our men and women in uniform who help protect our country and especially those who paid the ultimate sacrifice, which is why it has been said that "freedom is not free."

Just a friendly reminder, please help protect and preserve our planet and wildlife because God has entrusted us by giving us stewardship over it. So, let's save it. Thank you so much. May God bless you.

I believe this poem, "God's Beloved Country," needs to be integrated in our school system curriculum, targeting the Critical Race Theories and Black History Month. This short poem describes both the bad and good history of America in a nutshell, with a positive ending.

God's Beloved Country

"I salute the flag that represents the beloved country we all love so dear, that was formed with great tears, some of sadness, even from madness. But who can forget the times of gladness? When we unite despite our past, as fellow Americans for the common good, for liberty and justice for all, as one nation under God. Even though she's blemished from all her imperfections, she's still God's beloved country that sits on a shining hill that the whole world reveres."

~ R. S. Porter

May God Bless America!

ABOUT THE AUTHOR

Apostle R. S. Porter is the founder and pastor of The Church After God's Own Heart Inc., located in Chesapeake, VA. He is also the founder and president of Love Your Neighbor America (LYNA) www.lyna.org, a non-profit organization designed to help the poor and promote love, unity, and peace in America. Pastor Ray's comfort zone lies in preaching, evangelizing, helping people, and feeding the poor. He is family-oriented and enjoys swimming, boating, fishing, motorcycle riding, reading, and cooking. Above all, Pastor Ray loves preaching the gospel of Jesus Christ and seeing souls get saved. He prays and hopes that writing this book about topics that society normally avoids—yet that need to be addressed—would bring about dialogues across the world that will help start the healing process for many nations and people. And prayerfully, with God's intervention, we will establish a more God-fearing, unified America.

Let's show the world the God effect by making this book a household name. This is your call to action: Please be sure to spread the word about *The Tell-All Book: The Little Book God Wants the World to Read* with your friends on social media so that men may know God's plan for mankind concerning some of the topics in this book.

Thank you so much. God Bless You!

CPSIA information can be obtained
at www.ICGtesting.com
Printed in the USA
LVHW021203011122
732019LV00035B/805